The KPIs of Life

Copyright © 2025 by Will Everett
All rights reserved. No part of this book may be reproduced in any manner whatsoever without written permission except in the case of brief quotations embodied in critical articles and reviews.
First Printing, 2025

This book is dedicated to: my nephews – Khalil, Deuce, Kingston, and Zion; my god daughter, Baby Isla; and to my mother - for without her I wouldn't be here.

The KPIs of Life

Will Everett

Contents

Dedication	iii
You Ever Heard of Abraham Maslow?	1
KPI 1: Physical Health	10
KPI 2: Financial Health	23
KPI 3: Mental & Emotional Health	64
KPI 4: Relationship Health	96
KPI 5: Esteem Health	112
Where Self-Actualization Occurs	125
About the Author	129

You Ever Heard of Abraham Maslow?

The funny thing about life is that you don't always know if you're "doing it right". Sometimes you can feel like you're on top of the world and at other times it can feel like the whole world is on top of you. The famous Greek philosopher, Socrates, is often quoted as proclaiming that "an unexamined life is not worth living" – at least that's what I read within this book of quotes I kept on the toilet lid in my apartment at one time in life. At that time I was in the first year of my career and dealing with internal and external conflicts when I tapped into my unusually healthy habit of searching for inspiration whenever life got tough. The second I read that quote I made a conscious decision to examine my own life and this practiced lasted for just a couple of days. I would sit for moments at a time trying to recall my earliest memories. I reflected on the settings, the sounds, the scents, and whatever else would come to my mind or senses. I did this over and over again until I mentally transported to those time, all in pursuit of searching for something that would guide me through the challenging time I was in.

My reflections would often start with me at the tender age of six or seven. At that time I was just a kid in the south side of Chicago where I stayed with my sister, baby brother, five or six cousins at any given time, and our grandparents. I recalled snowy, windy walks from May St. to the local elementary school holding my grandmother and sister's hand. And as if it were within the same minute, I would recall the days when I was just a couple years older but now a visitor to that block. My cousins and I are walking to the corner store in the heat of summertime Chicago with two of my cousins alongside. We were in possession of grandma's EBT card and our minds full of dopamine induced joy that grew exponentially with every step we made on our journey to the corner store. At said corner store we were getting ready to splurge on candy, chips, juices, and whatever was on the list that grandma sent us off with. It's just a 2-minute walk around the corner but with my cousins it's an adventure through the world.

From there my memories drifted along chronological sequences of time until one day I recalled something that had me stuck in thought. I was in my Psychology 101 class in college and it came to me that it was around then that I formed the habit of searching for inspiration during troubling times. I connected this memory to my habit because it was in that class, at that moment, when I learned of something called "Maslow's Hierarchy of Needs". If you are not familiar with this Hierarchy of Needs concept then let me start by recognizing Maslow, because it was him – Abraham Maslow – who introduced me to it.

Back in the early 1940s a psychologist by the name of Abraham Maslow went searching for a methodical approach to achieving the greatest state of fulfillment in life. After conducting research and studies he came up with a theory of how humans can do this through what he described as 'fulfilling our Hierarchy of Needs'. This hierarchy consists of five specific levels of 'Needs' that I'll describe here from bottom up of this oft depicted pyramid.

Maslow's Hierarchy of Needs

Physiological Needs:
At the most basic level, or the base of this hierarchy, the theory suggests that all humans have *Physiological Needs* that intrinsically motivate us. Examples of our physiological needs are aspects of life like having water, good air quality, food, shelter, and means to reproduce. In fact, this level of needs is so essential that we would not be able to live very long if we could not sustain them. In other words, these basic needs are the closest things that we have to birth rights as a species. Without fulfilling this base level of Physiological Needs you'd be unable to function properly and even worse, it could be fatal.

Security Needs:
After meeting that base level of primal needs, Maslow's theory states that humans are then motivated by what he called *Security*

Needs which don't just speak to the feeling of personal security of self; it also speaks to having a means to secure those basic *Physiological Needs*. In other words, our security needs deal with our need to sustain a physical home to cover your head and shield your personal belongings; a car to get to and from places; and a consistent source of income to afford your standard of living, to name a few.

Love & Belonging Needs:

The third level of Maslow's Hierarchy of Needs is called our *Love & Belonging Needs*. This is where things begin to get a bit more complex and subjective. Along with survival and security all humans have a need to *belong* – this includes belonging within a family, a friendship, a romantic relationship, or any other form of connection amongst people. Scientifically it is proven that homo-sapiens (AKA us humans) are social creatures, although to what degree varies from person to person. Some people may find fulfillment in being by themselves most times while others would fall into a deep depression if they went more than a day without interacting with someone else. No matter the personality, though, this level of needs suggest that we are all motivated to sustain a sense of loving and being loved, or belonging. Said differently, this means that part of why us humans do what we do is for the purpose of having and maintaining some sense of love and community.

Esteem Needs:

Right below the peak state of Self-Actualization Maslow poses that, as humans, we are motivated by the need to be respected and of value if not by others, then by ourselves at least. He called this our *Esteem Needs* or the need to boost our self-esteem periodically. Whether that be due to our occupations, our abilities, our cache or some other distinguishing factor, Maslow's theory poses that on the journey to reach our penultimate state of fulfillment we all have a need to feel valued in some way and to feed our egos.

Self-Actualization Needs:

At the 5th and final level is the peak of Maslow's Hierarchy of Needs called *Self-Actualization Needs* and these needs are defined as the need to realize our greatest potential or to reach our highest level of fulfillment. This ideology poses that after, and only after, fulfilling those first 4 Needs to some degree can we begin fulfilling the need to reach our greatest potential in life. Generally speaking, without fulfilling the first four levels of needs one is unable to ever truly reach this level of self-actualization.

According to this theory of Maslow's Hierarchy of Needs if we can manage to fulfill each of these levels of needs then we can reach fulfillment in life. When I recalled the memory of learning about this it became a North Star for me to follow and from there I began a deep dive studying this theory in search of a framework that could guide me out of my depressed state at that time. Perhaps where I found Maslow to be most profound was in his disclaimer that these Needs – from Physiological to Self-Actualization – are never truly steady states. Instead, it should be inferred that they are transitory in nature. In a revision to his initial theory, years later Maslow categorized his five-level hierarchy into two broader buckets: Deficiency Needs (the first four levels on the Hierarchy of Needs) and Growth Needs (the self-actualization level). What I took from this split was the emphasis that the first four levels are basic to our survival and that if we wanted to do more than just survive then I would need to continuously work to sustain a level of fulfillment in those deficiency needs so that I could free up my capacity to actively drive my growth and development. Meaning self-actualization isn't some steady state of perfection that we work towards and then we have it forever. Instead, it is a steady state of continuous growth!

At the time of my reflection on Maslow's theory the internal conflict I had been dealing with was what can be best described as depressed and lost. My mother had just been imprisoned right as I graduated college and began my career and I felt the pain and fear of her situation while coping with a pressure to fill her shoes during this tragedy. Couple that with the anxiety of survivor's guilt and a growing sense of imposter's syndrome from feeling like I was just winging it as a first-time employee in Corporate America. On the outside was the façade of a young man with all the ambition in the world working towards a promising future. On the inside I was anxious, indecisive, and emotionally unstable.

I was working at one of the largest banks in the world yet every day I felt that I was not doing what I was supposed to be doing. I worked in this big office downtown, wore a suit and tie every day, and all of the elderly janitorial and security staff of the building would greet me with a big smile and call me 'Mr.' at 23 like I was someone important. While others spent their weekends doing what young professionals with money and no responsibilities do, I was spending my money flying three hours and driving another two hours to spend four hours a day visiting my mom in jail. I would come back to the office on Monday morning wearing a big smile and modestly brushing off my weekend as 'nothing major. Just relaxing really'. In retrospect, it wasn't as much a front as it was a coping mechanism for me to deal with the fact that I just felt I didn't belong and that no one was relatable to me in that season. In hindsight, though I felt I did not belong I was actually right where I needed to be at a time when I was searching for inspiration and purpose because I found both between my reflections on Maslow's Hierarchy of Needs and working in the Center of Excellence at Bank of America.

Most big corporations spend millions of dollars a year on collecting and analyzing data to reveal what are known as Key Performance Indicators or *KPIs*. A KPI is a metric that companies track on an ongoing basis to provide executives and stakeholders an indication of how the business is performing in specific areas, overall, and against peers. For Bank of America it was within that Center of Excellence team where they tracked their KPIs for each department under the company umbrella and for the enterprise as a whole. During my period of life examination, I made a connection between those KPIs that I was spending eight hours of my day analyzing and the Hierarchy of Needs I spent a few hours per night ruminating on. That realization changed the way I looked at life from then on which helped lift me out of crisis and an intentional path of continuous growth.

It dawned on me one day while working that KPIs were not exclusive to large enterprises and that all entities needed to determine and monitor their KPIs – including an entity of one. By contextualizing the levels on Maslow's Hierarchy of Needs in a way that was relevant to my everyday life I determined my own hierarchy of needs that I call the KPIs of Life. Through more examination and a little bit of trial and error these KPIs eventually became: Physical Health, Financial Health, Mental and Emotional Health, Relationship Health, and Esteem Health.

Maybe it was the engineer in me but the connection my brain made that day gave me liberating solace because it allowed me to view life in a way that could be measured, and just like with KPIs, if you can measure them you can monitor them and improve them. Before I curated these *Needs* into *KPIs* I simply focused on the Hierarchy as Maslow had laid out, I initially set my intentions on making sure that I had reached a level of mastery in my Deficiency Needs (the first four levels on the Hierarchy of Needs) and eventually working on my Growth Needs (the self-actualization level). Since then, by working to enhance my state within each step on Maslow's Hierarchy of Needs I have been able to fulfill my own KPIs of Life and achieve a level of success that I believe is attainable for all people.

As I made sense of this newfound perspective for myself I began examining my friends, family, and even strangers I encountered by asking them two questions: what would a better life look like for you in five years? Regardless of how they described it after thinking for a while, most people defined it as not just one thing in particular but a culmination of improvements to that Hierarchy of Needs Maslow introduced me to. I would hear things like "it would be..." driving the car they dreamt of having and living in the house of their dreams or being more secure financially or being married and with kids or being able to do what they love instead of what they feel like they have to.

The second question I would ask was: what would it take for you to grow? This question was much more difficult for people to answer and in their responses, or lack thereof, I identified a disconnect. People have a good idea of what they want the end state to look like but not many people had a clear picture of the journey it would take to get there. I realized that not many people related growth with success and that was a big lesson for me. In these surveys I was learning a lot about others but I also learned a lot about myself. Probing others gave me exposure to options of how my own life could look and as a byproduct I was able to realize Maslow's Hierarchy of Needs for myself through basic KPIs that anyone can track. What the following chapters detail is how the 21st century human being can fulfill their own Hierarchy of Needs through the five KPIs of Life. With a concerted focus on mastering these KPIs I believe that it is possible for anyone to create a clear path to self-actualization or, as I used to say, ensure a better life. Within these discrete KPIs of Life I wanted to also share the principles and practices that I implemented for myself to ensure that growth came from my efforts.

Like most things in life, it is the perspective that determines our perception and the perspective of success that I found by focusing on the health of my KPIs of Life instilled in me a concrete perception of success which made attaining it real. My hope is that from my perspective you receive at least a benchmark of what your perception of success should be. You may not have studied Maslow or sat in boardrooms discussing KPIs for hours – and I will leave it up to you to determine if you should or not – but in those avenues I found a road that the masses can take to success. Through the KPIs of Life what I am sharing is just one man's perspective of what it takes to take control of your own in life, to set goals for success, and to ultimately feel the fulfillment that comes from accomplishing those goals. That's all success is if you ask me – having a sense of control over your life by accomplishing your goals in such a way that enables you to have peak experiences and grow in life. Now let's journey into the KPIs, how you can master them, and ultimately grow into success!

KPI 1: Physical Health

If you think of the pyramid from the Hierarchy of Needs, the Physical Health KPI is the foundation of our KPIs of Life. Physical health refers to the overall state of an individual's physical wellness and the absence of disease or injury. It encompasses various factors such as physical fitness, nutrition, lifestyle habits, and management of any handicaps or deficiencies. Being physically healthy means having a body that is functioning well and able to perform daily activities. It involves having a healthy cardiovascular system; good muscular strength and endurance; healthy bones and joints; and a healthy body weight. What you can do to obtain and fulfill good physical health is as simple as following these key controls:

1. Eat a balanced and nutritious diet
2. Engage in regular exercise and physical activity
3. Get adequate rest and sleep
4. Avoid making habit of harmful activities such as smoking, alcohol consumption, and doing things with high risk of physical harm
5. Study your body

Health is truly wealth in this life because having it makes doing life much more pleasant and not having it makes life stressful, painful, costly, and less fulfilling. That's why adhering to these controls puts you in a position to do what you can control to fulfill good Physical Health. Now what about the detailed how? That part can be explained in a million ways by a million different people and half of them will be helpful or provide something to take heed to. But if you want to take my word I detail "how" you stay in good physical health like this:

Manage Your Diet:
Dr. Rupy Aujla, an NHS medical doctor and huge proponent of nutritional medicine, put it simply this way: "don't worry about changing your diet overnight. Just add one more colorful fruit and/or vegetable to your plate and eat it first. Start there." If you look online for "good diets" or "healthy diets" you will find a range from Mediterranean to Paleo to Vegan to Keto. At their core they're all good for the most part. They all support little to no processed foods, low trans fats and sugars, and high macronutrient intakes from whole foods predominately. Macronutrients are the nutrients that our bodies need in high doses in order to maintain homeostasis and function at it's most optimal state. More specifically, macronutrients are: proteins, carbohydrates, and fats. In the United States, the Food and Drug Administration actually requires that these macronutrients, or 'macros' for short, are included on the labels of all food items sold. So if you ever want to know what the protein, carbohydrate, and fat content is for the foods you eat simply look at the label on it's packaging.

The average female needs a caloric intake of 1800 to 2200 calories per day while the average male needs 2200 to 2500 calories per day. While these numbers can vary depending on an individual's physical fitness goals, a healthy intake of macronutrients means that at least 80 percent of those calories come from whole foods rich in these macros we laid out – proteins, carbohydrates, and fats. Just like with anything in life there are good macros and there are bad macros, which is why I place an emphasis on whole foods – the foods that are not processed and in their whole form (e.g., chicken breasts, vegetables, fruits, etc...). To make it easier to track, macros also have exact caloric ratios. For example, proteins and carbohydrates account for 4 calories per gram while fats account for 9 calories per gram.

In regards to healthy protein sources, this includes foods like tilapia, chicken breast, tofu, salmon, or lean beef or turkey in the meat section. In the dairy section healthy protein sources are foods such as eggs, Greek yogurt, and many cheeses just to name a few. In the legumes section these are food sources such as beans, lentils, and peas. If you can stock your kitchen with these foods you will have all the 'good' protein you need to sustain good Physical Health.

After your lean protein sources you should be adding healthy carbohydrates that are nutrient dense like vegetables and fruits. This list is much larger than the protein sources but some of the best fruits and veggies include, but are not limited to: spinach, carrots, broccoli, garlic, kale, beets, sweet potatoes, blueberries, apples, oranges, bananas, avocado, and watermelon. These foods are packed with healthy carbohydrates, vitamins, and other micronutrients and minerals that are good for maintaining peak homeostasis within the body.

One note to make regarding these foods is that you should not substitute the concentrate or juice version of these fruits and veggies. While certainly not a bad substitute, juices are not the same as whole foods because whole foods are what pack the highest volume of nutrients. The concentrate form of fruits and vegetables are often depleted of some of the nutrients and minerals and when bought in juice form off the shelf they almost always include other chemicals and preservatives to preserve the shelf life that aren't necessarily optimal for our bodies. What you put inside of your body is truly medicine or poison so understand what you're consuming by reading the food labels. If you don't know what an ingredient is look it up and educate yourself of what it does inside of the body.

Now for the fats. Most of those healthy sources of proteins and carbs also contain healthy sources of fat as well so as long as you are eating healthy sources of proteins and carbs you are likely also eating healthy sources of fat (e.g., cheeses, avocados, meats). All three of these macronutrients work within the body to keep up everyday functions like having energy to do things, maintaining hormone levels, and boosting the immune system to fend off sicknesses and diseases. This is why I consider food to be medicine! Healthy food provides the natural enhancements your body needs to fend off unwanted substances while unhealthy, processed, and high sugar and sodium foods stunt the body's natural ability to keep the body and mind in peak shape. As the saying goes: *"it's not on you, it's in you"*. So put good things in your body (for a sustained period of time) and not only will it show on the outside but you will feel better internally as well. For comparison, developing a bad diet can often lead to high blood sugar, diabetes, cancers, and other critical health conditions that negatively impact your quality of life. Everything from our physical health to mental health are all impacted by the foods we consume so keep that in mind as you make your meal selections.

When most people think of a diet they often skip the part about fluids but the most important liquid you can put in your body is water, which makes up about 60% of the human body. It not only keeps us hydrated but it also serves as our body's natural lubricant much like oil in an engine or the Earth for that matter. Water is also our body's natural conduit to circulate nutrients and remove wastes. To that extent, a good diet should consist of at least 64 oz of water per day which equates to 8 cups. Adequate water intake positively influences the body's natural energy levels and physical functions; it aids in weight maintenance; and it helps maximize mental performance. So on top of consuming quality foods be sure to prioritize consuming water before, if not to completely replace, all other liquids. As an easy best practice reward yourself with a cup every hour that you are awake!

There are certainly supplements to enhance a good diet to great but I want you to grow, not be perfect. What I have provided are the core fundamentals that promote a good diet so as long as you follow a diet with these tenets incorporated you are controlling a key aspect of your Physical Health. Too often, especially in America, we shove our faces with processed and fast foods, quick meals and drinks high in sugars, artificial preservatives, trans fat, and sodium. These are ok if consumed in moderation – three or four times per month - but unfortunately this is what many people consume three or four times per day! That's called out of control and being out of control with our diet can significantly increase the likelihood of disease caused by malnutrition. So, it's ok to be human and given in to our guilty pleasure of junk food here and there but it should seriously be limited and accounted for in your physical activity, which leads us to the next control for good Physical Health.

Manage Your Activity:

Now that you are powering up your body with good fuel the goal of powering something is to use it, right? Well with our bodies it is no different. Have you ever heard the saying "if you don't use it you lose it"? Well, that pertains to the body as well. While a good diet is the foundation of good physical health, exercise and physical activity are essential for optimizing that perfectly fueled body. Don't just take my word for it, though. According to Health.gov "regular physical activity is one of the most important things people can do to improve their health. Moving more and sitting less have tremendous benefits for everyone, regardless of age, sex, race, ethnicity, or current fitness level." While genealogy does play a significant role in your body's makeup, adhering to a good diet and putting your body through challenging physical activity serve a much more significant role in your overall physical well-being. According to the CDC, regular physical activity is a key proponent to fending off diseases and disorders such as diabetes, arthritis, and many cardiovascular irregularities. Moreover, physical activity has been linked to better mental health as well as having the ability to release endorphins like dopamine, commonly referred to as the "happy hormone".

Since I can remember I have been involved in sports. From peewee football all the way to college I've played sports and even after college I've remained active. According to the 2nd Edition of the Physical Activity Guidelines for Americans, published by Health.gov, that puts me in the 80th percentile of Americans who get regular physical activity. This is no self-absorbing statistic on my behalf, rather, it is an eye opener to reality. Out of the 195 countries that this world is comprised of, the USA is in first place for obesity and deaths due to cancer as of 2023. As the greatest country in the world that is a disheartening data point. The combination of how little we work out as a society and how much processed and fast-food we consume leads us to also standout in the category of highest population of unhealthy people. This is no coincidence. It's science. Diets high in processed fats, sugars, and sodium can lead to chronic inflammation and metabolic stress. This creates an environment in the body that may promote the development of diseases, including some forms of cancer. This kind of stuff happens at the molecular level and shows up in the way we look and how our bodies function.

If you're new to physical activity and good diets don't feel that you have to move to a perfect state overnight but do start forming good habits immediately! There's a popular saying that "Rome wasn't built in one night" and neither will having excellent physical health so, I know it always sounds easier to say than do, try not to focus on the end of your work – just try to enjoy the process of growing a KPI into great health. I'm a big fan of starting with small steps that can be kept up with. Find the parking spot furthest from the door. Swap out sitting at a bar with friends for taking walks with friends. Replace a fast food meal with a home cooked meal; remove all of the sodas and juices from your grocery trip for a month and commit to only water instead. Next time you find yourself with nothing to do go for a light jog or hit the gym. It's little changes in our daily decisions like this that can make a world of difference when you are just starting out to become active.

There are tons of resources in books, online, and through word of mouth that can help you generate ideas to stay active physically and eat cleaner. I've shared only but a few and, truth be told, a few is all you need if you can commit to making them habits. So remember this as you journey on your path to control your Physical Health. There is a lot of life that is out of our control but I have found great success in not just identifying my Key Performance Indicators in life but identifying the things I can control to enhance the health of them.

Manage Your Rest:

Sticking with the analogy of the body being a battery powered machine, using that machine results in draining it's battery. Just as you would plug your phone or laptop up to a charger to replenish it's juice the human body is no different. It has to recharge and the way human bodies recharge and replenish is through rest. Notice I say, replenish, though. When you plug up your phone or laptop it doesn't just refill it's charge. In some cases it does updates or reconfigures or resets the entire system to do more! That's the value of maintaining a healthy sleep regimen and why getting adequate sleep is a control to your Physical Health KPI.

If I can be honest I will tell you that I was not always the best at getting adequate rest. I used to live by this ideology that I had to "earn my sleep" and "take no days off" but this was a cancerous ideology to overall good physical health. Sleep is the cornerstone of good physical health and thus equally, if not more important, than a good diet or physical activity. Now will you have a few all-nighters in your life? Well, I think any life of ambition is susceptible to that, but let's not mistake those few rare occasions with good, steady habits.

The benefits of sleep are well researched and vast. From muscle recovery and fighting off sickness to healthy neurological and cardiovascular functionality, sleep impacts nearly every aspect of our body and overall well-being. Most research states that eight hours of sleep per night is considered quality sleep so this is an easy control to manage. If you find it hard getting eight hours I challenge you to do three simple things every day.

1. The moment you wake up, set an alarm for eight hours before you have to wake up the next day. This establishes your 'bed time'.
2. Cut off consuming all food and drink at least one hour before that bed time. This gets the body ready to be inactive.
3. Move your phone to the furthest part of your room before you get in bed at your bed time and ensure the room is dark and cool. This helps keep you from distracting the body from doing what it is built to do at bed time.

Taking these steps day in and day out will help you form the habits you need to control your sleep. I will never stop emphasizing that good health is never an overnight process, it's a multinight process. The true test in each of the KPIs of Life is in our ability to be disciplined enough to do just a few things consistently. Getting adequate sleep is one of the easier things for us to control (unless, of course, you have a medical condition), so make this a quick win by prioritizing getting your sleep under control.

Knowledge of Self:

"An unexamined life is not worth living". Remember that quote? As stern as it may come to some, I hope that it resonates enough to allow you the time to reflect because without examining yourself, how do you know how you are doing? When it comes to your Physical Health it is not enough to say that you have good health because you feel like it. You have to study your body to really 'know'. That is why studying the body is the last control that we must manage to ensure we have good Physical Health.

Your body is constantly changing throughout a lifetime, with some changes occurring more frequently and more noticeably than others. For example, cellular turnover – a natural and essential process that the body undergoes to maintain, function, and repair our tissues – this happens everyday but you would never notice by observing day by day. Or something like bone mass. It peaks around the age of 30 and then gradually declines leading to changes in bone density and strength over time. If not controlled it can lead to chronic pain, increased fracture risk, or a bone disease like osteoporosis. Hormone levels also change throughout life, with significant shifts occurring during puberty (generally adolescence or teenage years), pregnancy and menopause for women (generally 55+), and with aging and a sedentary lifestyle in men.

All these reasons give insight for why it is important to your Physical Health KPI that you go get regular checkups on your body.

Physicals are key as an adult. Having a medical professional check your vitals and conduct bloodwork for you is quintessential to monitoring and managing your Physical Health KPI. Unless you are medically trained it is fair to say that it is not natural to be an expert in the body. While everyone's body is different, our bodies are also extremely homogenous. For geeks' sake, this is proven. All humans share more than 99% of the same DNA; with rare exceptions, of course, everyone has the same 206 bones, the same major organs and muscle systems (circulatory, respiratory, nervous, etc); and we all rely on the same cellular processes. This is why understanding as much about your body from an expert as you can is so valuable. If you pay attention to it, you are an expert on your body in your own right but for more technical analysis like bloodwork and screenings, that should be administered by a doctor.

As soon as I started working in Corporate America I took notice to my health benefits since it was the first time that I had my own medical insurance.

Pro Tip: If you are starting off in a job always ask for insight on the health benefits your employer offers.

I learned that virtually all health plans allow at least one free annual physical per year so I started there by just getting my first physical that summer. During an annual physical a doctor checks all of the vitals like heart rate, blood pressure, various reflexes, eye sight, and upon request, they can draw your blood to reveal helpful metrics and information about your body and it's performance.

Another Pro Tip: get bloodwork at least once per year.

I am grateful I had the kind of mother to make me go to the dentist every year but other than that, the only time I saw a doctor growing up is when I needed shots for school or had an injury in sports. Because of this I wasn't completely lost at what was going on but I was curious about anything thing she used to evaluate me. I asked my doctor dozens of questions starting with "why", "what", and "how"?

- Why are you drawing blood?
- Why do you test my heart rate and blood pressure?
- What can you tell me about myself from drawing my blood?
- What does a good heart rate look like? What about blood pressure?
- How does this thing squeezing my arm work?
- How do I make sure I have a good heart rate and blood pressure?

Questions like these were how I probed her and when I received my report back from my doctor I began to focus on it like a KPI scorecard because that's what it looked like to me. Just a sheet full of rows that indicated the parameter being tested and columns that provided the value of the corresponding row. At that point I grew more curious about how to interpret the numbers or values and luckily I had a helpful (and patient) doctor who helped me to do that. This helped me to learn about the things I could do to keep my body in a state that wasn't just good because I thought it was, but good because I had a way to test both seen and unseen parts of my body. If I hit within the range of values that doctors suggest, then I was in good Physical Health. I learned which values indicate problems with different organs or bodily functions and which parameters were based more on genes than habits. To this day I prioritize getting a yearly physical and at this point it is not just one data point but a progress report that I can use to adjust my habits if I need to.

If you have health insurance typically your provider pays for one visit so all you have to do is schedule an appointment with a physician that is within your insurance's network and get there. If you do not have insurance and you cannot take advantage of a decreased copay rate be diligent in looking for free resources throughout your local city. I hope this ages well, but many cities have community clinics and non-profit centers that offer free physicals, screenings, and bloodwork. This control could be the sole difference between us having good or bad Physical Health as it is both a detective measure and a preventive one. While I cannot quantify an exact number, I can say that most illnesses to the body can be prevented. If you can prevent bad Physical Health why wouldn't you?

The importance of examining your life to manage it cannot be overstated and not just when it comes to your health. The transferable skill here is that much like in school or on a car's dashboard, numbers and values can really tell you a lot. Consistent A's tells you that you've really been grasping the information shared in class. Seeing your fuel level percentage on your dashboard tells you how far you have to go before you need to refill or else suffer potential breakdowns or damage to your car. If you can measure it, you can typically improve it, and if you can improve it you should. So getting a physical or semi-annual check up isn't just a nice to have benefit, it is truly necessary to ensuring a good Physical Health KPI.

The infamous GOAT NFL cornerback and football coach, Deion Sanders, is quoted having said, "if you look good, you feel good; if you feel good, you perform great". He was responding to why he dressed up flashy for football games, but nevertheless his response is universally effective. What he implied by saying this as an athlete performing at the highest level is: the looking, feeling, and performing happens with intention. Doing good by your body so that it can look and feel good are key inputs that allow you to perform at your peak level, thus serving as a catalyst for achieving your consistent peak experiences in life. Here's the proof: ask anyone if they can recall when they were in the best shape of their lives. Almost everyone could tell you in great detail and I bet you they smile while recalling all of the great experiences associated with that time period.

If any of what was just discussed seems overwhelming or intimidating, don't fret and don't underestimate the value of the times in which we live. It has never been easier to learn things – search credible websites and blogs, check out podcasts on the subject, talk to your network about it. If you need help starting, you have everything you need in what you just read – a good diet, consistent physical activity, adequate sleep, and consistent health screenings or checkups. Practicing these few things will impact everything about your life and practicing them with discipline and consistency will result in improvements in your body and overall physical health. In return you will find more gratification and get one step closer towards truly sustaining a life of consistent peak experiences and growth that defines self-actualization for you. Just as in business, the health of our KPIs isn't just a checkbox – it's a daily practice. The more you control your controls the better your health and with a solid foundation in your Physical Health KPI all other KPIs in life become easier to build on.

KPI 2: Financial Health

If you ask me, taking care of one's body is primal and of greatest importance for any human being so that is why I call it the foundational KPI. It is hard for anything to be worthwhile if our physical health is bad, but good physical health is an act of self-preservation. If you are reading this from anywhere on planet Earth, though, it is likely that even self-preservation of physical health is not free for you. To understand what I mean consider the following stats. According to the Federal Reserve's Survey of Consumer Finances from 2022, which provides insights into American households' finances, the median amount of savings for all American families is $7,000 (*the median is a better indicator than the average as it excludes the ultra-wealthy outliers*). To dive deeper, it also has the data to show that the average American approximately spends:

- 33% of their income on providing a roof for themselves (e.g., rent/mortgage, light bills, water, etc...);
- 15% of transportation costs (car note, insurance, gas, etc....);

- another 15% on feeding themselves (groceries, dining out, etc...);
- and about 10% on health and Medicare (taxes, insurance, regular checkup additions, ad-hoc visits, etc...).

That's exactly 73% of the average American's monthly income spending on providing a living. Now let's consider those four categories to be the minimum of what is needed in order to say that you have fulfilled those basic physiological and security needs, as Maslow categorizes them. I simply call me the basic needs to make a living. I think we can all agree that healthcare is necessary for adequate well-being so that expense makes sense. As we mentioned in the prior chapter, being able to feed one's self, let alone properly, is primal and thus also necessary for adequate well-being. Sure, getting around by bus is an affordable alternative in most major cities but I am going to say that it's not a far-fetched idea that a basic (again, 'Western') necessity for adequate well-being is the capability to get around at will. Thus having a car that is in working condition is a necessity so becomes money to maintain it's condition. And lastly, we won't belabor this point but safe to say that our biggest monthly expense – rent or mortgage payments – is of course quintessential to sustaining our physiological and safety needs by definition.

Now let's conduct a quick *back of the napkin* analysis to make this real. I googled "average monthly income in America" and after searching several sites I landed on CEICdata.com, a 30-year-old company that specializes in capturing and analyzing macroeconomic data. This source showed that the average American, as of July 2023, made:

- $80,610 per year before taxes and deductions

THE KPIS OF LIFE 25

- Divide that number by 12 and you get a monthly pay of $6,717 per month (again, before taxes and deductions)
- Now let's, for example, assume that the person earning this income lives in a state with no income taxes so all this person had to pay was federal income taxes at an effective tax rate of 11.8% when you consider a standard deduction of about $15,000 (the 2025 standard deduction amount).
- Now by multiplying that $6,717 by (1-.118) you get $5,924 and some change
- For sake of completely boring with the math here, let's just assume that this is really the baseline number from which that 73% is coming from. I felt this piece necessary to sketch out because taxes often take up a material chunk of money for the average person. Too much to not account for and in this case close to 12%!

For this average person who brings home $5,924 per month after taxes, if 73% in living expenses is deducted from that, that means they keep just about $1,600 for themselves each month. If I just focus on that number that's left over then I deduce that either the average American is not doing too great at saving or that those living expenses are low-ball estimates. If I focus on reality, though, I would say that it's a little bit of both and that's where the KPIs of Life come in.

I spent the majority of my life obtaining knowledge by exposing myself to the world around me, journeying to understand everything in a way that made sense to me, and seeking to learn from every person and experience I came in contact with. One of the greatest learnings I've had, and continue to have, is the exposure and learning of a subject that is known as financial acumen. Financial acumen is the understanding of finances in a way that you can use – with the key word here being *use*! What I learned has been essential to how myself and so many others fulfill our Hierarchy of Needs, from our Physiological Needs to Self-Actualization Needs. The principles and practices I have developed can serve as a pragmatic foundation for anyone on their journey of making the best out of their everyday reality. The principles are:

1. Keep a healthy relationship with money
2. Know what's valuable and become valuable
3. Live by budgeting
4. Invest early and invest often

So, What Is a Healthy Relationship With Money?
If you buy into the idea that a relationship is any recurring interaction between any two or more entities – be it human and food, human and human, or a human and money – then a healthy relationship with money is one that has the makings of a healthy relationship with just about anything else.

- It has consistently positive interactions;
- it promotes growth;
- and it does, in some way, mutually aid self-preservation.

These three components are the cornerstones of any healthy relationship and thus the cornerstones of a healthy relationship with money. A healthy relationship with money starts with a growth mindset around the utility of money and ends with how we execute on that mindset.

You see, the natural purpose of money is to serve as a utility. By definition a utility is something designed to be used and as we mentioned above, we know money has to be used to live. The thing is – the average person doesn't just want to live; we want to live fulfilled! Think about it, no one says "I *just* want to make money". Normally it follows a *"so what"* – "so I can buy a new car", "so I can buy mom her dreamhouse", or "so I can make it out of my town". This desire to use money to live a more fulfilling life is human nature. We have our basic needs but we also have desires and this is ok under the condition we utilize money to positively interact with, promote growth, and aid in our self-preservation along the way.

Enjoying the fruits of one's labor is something I believe we are all entitled to when we work to make an honest living, but unfortunately many people exhaust that full paycheck they bring home after taxes instead of utilizing it in a healthy way. This is why 65% of Americans live paycheck to paycheck, at risk of financial insecurity, according to the 2025 'Paycheck to Paycheck' report from the sites 'PYMNTS' and 'LendingClub'. This implies that for most Americans the 73% in "living expenses" is probably more like 80-85% with the remaining likely used for those desires or paying even more for the living expenses that the average. If this is the case then the harsh reality is that most of America has an unhealthy relationship with money.

And that's not just a financial issue. Beyond the obvious threat to meeting our Physiological and Safety Needs, there's a growing body of research connecting Financial Health to Physical Health. My college science teacher used to say, "correlation doesn't equal causation," but there's overwhelming evidence that financial insecurity—not having enough money to reliably pay your bills—is strongly correlated with both mental and physical health issues. The more uncertain we are about making ends meet, the more likely we are to suffer from depression, anxiety, and even cardiovascular disease. This is why Financial Health is the second KPI in the KPIs of Life, and why building a healthy relationship with money isn't just smart—it's essential.

Money is what we work for, it's what we spend, and it's what we leverage, but for what purpose is always the true question. The answer to that question is what plays the biggest part in our Financial Health. Some people spend money on investments, some on clothes, some on self-improvement, some on that extra guac and Starbucks every day. If you show me someone's bank statement I can (with a high degree of certainty) tell you a lot about their relationship with money. Does their bank account indicate good financial acumen or a poor financial acumen?

A bank account that shows poor financial acumen is one that is constantly used for things that gain no value over time. You would only see items like: club charges, frequent dining out spend, excessive fashion buys, and other materialistic things just used for consumption. The bank statement of someone with good financial acumen, on the other hand, would include things like: transfers to investment accounts, pretty consistent grocery store purchases, withdrawals for books, travel, gym memberships, etc. In other words it shows that their money is being utilized to grow, improve, and preserve their life in some way. That there is quintessential to being not just financially healthy but financially free.

For me, that was the goal of developing a healthy relationship with money – freedom. After seeing enough unhealthy relationships with money and even repeating some of the unhealthy habits myself I changed my mindset and began to focus my energy on gaining knowledge about finance and how to use money to improve my financial position. Similarly, I would recommend to anyone the same – determine what your goal for Financial Health is so that it can drive your discipline for keeping a healthy relationship with money. This discipline is the foundation of our Financial Health KPI so control it like your life depends on it because it just might.

'Finance' is just a word but in real life it describes anything to do with how money works thus financial acumen is simply having knowledge to understand how money works and make smart decisions within your finances. If you are anything like me then you probably weren't taught how to make smart decisions with your money. I wasn't born with a Finance degree or a trust fund entitled to me and I didn't grow up having conversation about finances at the dinner table. It's no coincidence that the kids of successful people are often themselves successful and it's certainly no happenstance that someone who is born with equitable assets to their name has a leg up on someone who wasn't.

So how do you build financial acumen if you weren't born into it? The same way we build any new skill – exposure and education. The good news is that with a little curiosity and a lot of discipline, acquiring new skills has never been easier. You don't need a trust fund or a finance degree, you can search Google or listen to finance podcasts like 'Earn Your Leisure' to get exposure to financial acumen. Even better news is that you can learn all the good habits you'll need to sustain a good Financial Health KPI right here in the rest of this chapter!

My Exposure to Money

If you're reading this, I'm going to assume that you find it common sense to say you've got to have money in the first place in order to use it. If you happened to not know, though, there are more ways than ever to get money in these days of the 21st century. Let me do my part in providing exposure by listing plainly a few simple ways here:

- Jobs in Corporate America
- Drive Uber
- Rent products

- Consult
- Sell a service
- Create a product to sell (offline and online)
- Teaching people a skill
- Take pictures
- Create content
- Going to college (much more on this later)

These are just a few of the countless ways to earn money. Take a second to think about what these things have in common, though. If you gave that some thought, hopefully some word synonymous with 'providing a service' or 'serving' came to mind. That's the key. Making money is all about how and in what capacity you can serve and, more specifically, how can you serve in a capacity that someone would want or need to pay for.

In my life I have lived in government housing, large single-family homes, and even slept in a car. I have seen the inside of a prison and I have also seen in the inside of boardrooms and sat right across from billionaires. I have failed classes and been at risk of getting kicked out of college but I eventually walked across the stage for a college degree twice! I have lived periods of life where my bank account was constantly in overdraft and I eventually progressed to not having to worry about even looking at my bank account because I know there's always something there.

Seeing as how life panned, at a young age I realized the truth in the great poet, Kanye West's enlightening words when he said, 'having money is not everything; not having it is'. I learned that money didn't replace morals but I also observed that those with it had a better quality of life overall; I learned that money didn't replace family but saw that you could do more for that family with it; and I knew that money did not replace the sheer value of a person but I also observed how it somehow makes some people treat you different. These realizations opened up my mind to become curious about money so you can say that those realizations are what allowed me to yearn for exposure to making money.

When I got to high school in 2006 I got my first laptop and I remember getting on *Ask Jeeves* (google that if you don't know lol) to search "How to get a lot of money?" At the top of the list of results was this list that US Weekly published called the '100 Best Paying Jobs List'. As the name suggests, this was a ranked list of the top 100 occupations by yearly salary and it also went into the difference between salary and take-home pay which was extremely useful context for me. Because of this, even though she did not talk to us about money, I extrapolated that my mom's job as a CPA was landing her between $60-$70,000 a year at that time (which was about 20% higher than the median salary in 06'). With this I also knew that Uncle Sam and healthcare were taking about 25% of that and that bills, gas, groceries, and other necessities were taking 30% of the remainder. I also knew that my two siblings and I took up about another 25% throughout the year just keeping us provided for in various ways.

That simple understanding at the age of 14 empowered me to seek a part-time job that way I could pay for my own $7.50 movie ticket on the weekends or my $2 Whataburger meal every morning before for school and sometimes the shoes I wanted when I could save up enough. Exposure to high paying jobs put me on a path that made me take school seriously as the exposure to that list also taught me that they all required a college degree of some sort. My curiosity in getting to college gave me the additional exposure of what differentiated colleges from one another which then made me curious about what impacted my acceptance into colleges like Harvard and Yale versus what I would need to enroll in a community college. With my new found knowledge I grew the desire to attend the best college and with the exposure my curiosity allowed me to gain it propelled me to pick up extra-curriculars in high school. I joined other extra-curriculars like sports, student government, and even studied Latin because I read that these things made me a more attractive candidate to the most prestigious college institutions.

The beauty of seeking exposure is that if you're hungry enough you will almost always find something of value, even on accident. Everything that I was exposed to about getting into college came as a byproduct of wanting exposure to how I could make money and I share that story as a real example of what it looks like to seek and gain exposure consistently. My exposure advanced even further when I transferred to a college prep school before my junior year of high school. This part of life was a whole new world for me and though it was a bit intimidating at first, the same desire to gain exposure to whatever could advance me towards making money propelled me even further.

In order to get what you have never had you have to do what you have never done. That has been the story of my own life but also the story of many people who are financially healthy. Achieving success at anything often means walking into unknown territories at some point, if not most times. I credit my advantages in life to the ironic fact that I actually felt so disadvantaged for most of my life, especially early on, because I often walked in places unfamiliar to me without much guidance. I was doing things that no one else around me was doing which meant I often had to do it alone. Or so it felt like it. That's what it felt like when I went to prep school initially, when I entered college, and even when I started my career. Luckily I had all the exposure I needed to develop myself.

Exposure + Skill Development = Value

Deciding to attend prep school after my sophomore year in a public high school was yet another byproduct of my initial exposure to wanting to learn how to make money. My mother shared with me this school called Greenhill College Prep in Dallas, TX – about a 45-minute drive from my neighborhood. Like most prep schools they required a great GPA and the passing of a standardized test in order to attend. She knew that I was eager to attend college because not only did I have exposure but more importantly I was doing the work to be a good candidate. By the age of 16 I was enrolled in a full AP curriculum at my high school, I had a 4.0 GPA, and I was a varsity athlete in two sports.

In my two years of high school I developed my test taking skills well enough to seize the opportunity she afforded me so much so that when I applied to Greenhill I tested well enough to be accepted on a full ride scholarship (the fact that my family was considered 'low income' on paper played a part in this as well). This set me on a trajectory to turn all that I was exposed to into opportunities to develop further because other than my part time jobs this was the first time in life where I got to see how well certain skills paid. Getting accepted into a top prep school in high school was rewarding enough but knowing that my mother wouldn't have to pay $30,000 per year for me to do so showed me first-hand the power of developing valuable skills.

Over the next two years I spent my time getting exposure from teachers who were more devoted to my education than I experienced in public school. The extra curriculars in prep school afforded me opportunities to travel the country and even accomplish my first big goal of attending Harvard for summer school before graduating. The kids I was surrounded by now talked about a lot more than just sports and provided just the challenge I needed to develop even further. The thing is, even with my exposure, the plan I formulated in high school did not go exactly according to plan and little did I know that development was really just getting started for me.

Because of that exposure in high school I knew that in college I'd be eligible for summer internships at corporations so long as I kept a decent GPA. I also knew that internships were paid, but it was not until my first summer of college that I would learn that the sheer fact of being a student studying a STEM field would make me eligible for opportunities simply because most of the companies desired students with analytical skills – skills often assumed (and in fairness, mostly proven) to be learned, practiced, and honed in a STEM based curriculum. And just as in high school, I discovered that being a student-athlete who had extracurricular involvement on campus afforded you even more opportunities. All of this exposure continuously played into my development as I matriculated through college.

During my first summer of college I decided to take an internship offer that was local and not very well paid because I wanted to spend most of my time working out with my team mates in preparation for the upcoming football season. That fall, though, my peers came back with hundreds of shared stories of how their internships went and through their stories I grew a deeper desire to get in the game of interning. While I stayed local earning just $200 per week teaching middle schoolers in order to better my chances of playing time, I learned that many of my peers were making $200 per day to develop skills that would pay them a lot more upon graduation.

The benefit of being in college was that I had the opportunity of researching and learning from like-minded classmates and staff about the 'best' companies to work for and what skills it would take to become employed by them. Whatever company they exposed me to I would go to the company website, read their 'About' section and then research what internships they were offering. In most cases they disclosed the salaries so I naturally sought out requirements of the highest paying jobs. This was the key exposure that guided my decision making academically and what organically guided my development. The requirements were often written out in a sentence that described what the job would entail and in other cases they were listed plainly as subjects.

If it was a subject that was already a part of my curriculum like 'engineering' or 'Calc II' or 'VBA coding' I would pay extra close attention to those lectures in class and spend time with people who knew the application of the skills I was learning. If it were a skill that was not in my curriculum like 'financial modeling' or 'cost benefit analysis' I would talk to friends who were studying those subjects and study with them to gain exposure and develop some level of skill. I wasn't focused on being an expert; I just wanted to know enough to determine what was useful in my pursuit of a high-paying internship.

By the end of my four-year journey through college I had researched hundreds of top companies, exposed myself to dozens of high paying skills and high paid individuals through interviews, and eventually developed those skills and relationships through real world exposure. By the time I graduated I knew how to add value because I had exposure to high value skills and I developed them with intention. That's it; that's the caption. Intentional exposure breeds intentional development and where those two intentions meet you will always find value.

Now I don't know where you are in your life journey but I do know there is always time and a way to find value. It simply requires exposing yourself to the world around you and seeking to do more within it. For me, I wanted to be more than a broke college student; I wanted to be able to take care of myself and my family adequately; I wanted to be someone that did not need financial help but instead could give it. I wanted to experience true freedom! I also knew that this meant I needed money for all of that so I exposed myself to ways to make the most of it by developing my skills in college. It didn't hurt that I also found multiple ways to make money while in college as a teacher's assistant, a tutor, and working off campus on the weekends.

The Truths About Developing Skills

The truth is that developing skills doesn't come naturally to most people. In fact, I don't believe it comes naturally to anyone. What I failed to mention before is that somewhere between wanting to get into the best and actually doing what was necessary in high school, I fell in love with football. I still wanted a good job and determined that college was the way but I also built up the dream that college would prolong my football career. So even though college was my pursuit my passion was football, not obtaining high paying skills.

There was no such thing as a paid internship to play football, though, so while fulfilling my love of playing football I also maintained the mindset of fulfilling my desire to have good Financial Health. Luckily for me, I attended Morehouse College where being well-rounded was emphasized and exposure to so much was right at my fingertips. Though it was not an overnight success story, the journey of exposure and development inevitably taught me a key aspect in my pursuit of a high paying career – what companies spend money on and what they make money doing. With that knowledge it became a simple question of what was I willing to do to either help them spend or make that money. I saw that at the intersection of a need gap and my willingness to fill it was an opportunity for me to convert my resume full of exposure and skills developed into value that resonated with a company.

Companies need employees so you can learn how a company is organized and what they need employees for and serve the needs of that company. Or maybe you realize that people need something that you yourself can provide so you study courses or watch YouTube videos and market yourself as a professional at serving that clientele. If you happen to have a cell phone there are ample ways to make money through marketing, influencing, reviewing things, servicing and selling things, and so much more all from the palm of your hand.

I was never someone that learned everything I needed to learn by listening to my professor's lecture for an hour. I almost always had to read the textbook, attend tutoring sessions, talk to people more experienced, and surf YouTube or the internet for every possible question that ever came to mind and it was through those processes that I picked up skills like VBA coding, which helped me land first full-time job at the largest retail bank in the country even though I never took one Finance class.

It was also that same routine that taught me about investment banking and how to model financial statements which gave me the skills I needed to then pivot to investment banking at one of the most prestigious investment banks in the world. I emphasize this because gaining exposure and development is often a process and does not occur overnight, unfortunately. Hardly ever is it just one thing that you are exposed to and develop that generates value in reality. More often than not it is a lot of exposure along with the combination of skills development that makes the most impactful value add situations for us. That's another truth.

If you have the capacity to learn a valuable skill then you have the capacity to use your knowledge to earn a living. While it is very easy to say this, I recognize that the willingness and appetite to experience new things varies from person to person, and that is fine. I also realize that everyone's capabilities vary based on various factors, some out of our control. I wish that I was a 6'10 guy with a 40-inch vertical and great basketball skills because I'd certainly be shooting to play in the NBA but my genes did not qualify me that way so I found other things that I enjoy to make a fulfilling living.

I spent most of my childhood with a speech impediment and I only overcame it by forcing myself to read books out loud and speak publicly via Toastmasters classes and eventually in front of crowds. That took years, though. I unfortunately know of no ways to snap your fingers and magically have every high value skillset on Earth but I do know the sure way to acquire skills is through consistent exposure to and development of them. The earlier you start the better but more importantly, the earlier you start the more likely it is that a passion is found in that same routine of exposure and development! Rather than try to write a book about all the skills you can gain and jobs you could obtain with them here's a list of mostly free resources to learn and develop high-value skills:

- YouTube
- Coursera
- Udemy
- Khan Academy
- Google

Now if you can spend time doing nothing but gaining skills that would be ideal, but if you're juggling the realities of life and it's responsibilities like practically everyone else then you have to carve out time to prioritize learning and honing highly sought after high-value skills. The last truth is that this is not a one and done activity either as the world is constantly changing. People's needs, economies, the trends, are all constantly changing so you must develop a growth mindset and become a life-learner. With a growth mindset you not only see money as a utility to grow but you also everything around you as an opportunity to grow.

With exposure and skills you are equipped to adopt the principle of always seeking to serve by providing value. Trying to learn how to make money and then how to get into college and then how to gain top paying internships gave me that exposure. I built a strong set of high-value skills not by choice, but because each year the skills required changed so I, too, had to change. If you can adopt this principle of finding value and becoming valuable you will never be without money for long and what's more, so many other opportunities will open up for you to sustain Financial Health.

While it can be a lofty upfront investment, the beauty of college is that you get to leverage time spent there for a wide array of exposure and even better you get to do so with hundreds or thousands of others that you can lean on to advance and aid your development. That's why, if you ask me, the greatest get rich quick scheme I know is to spend time in college (or life otherwise) to develop and learn to leverage high value skills. To be clear, college is not the only way to learn what skills are valuable. There is a lot of real-life experience that college simply cannot teach so while I have my experience as proof of value, there are many other ways to learn and develop the skills to keep you valuable. You just have to develop that childlike curiosity to expose yourself to them throughout life.

I will leave it to you to find your purpose, your calling, or simply the thing that you enjoy doing for money. It can be multiple things and it can change as the seasons; so long as you are growing through exposure and developing valuable skills gaining money will be well within reach for you. Since money is a utility, whatever you do with it, prioritize building and maintaining a healthy relationship with it. The foundation of that relationship is budgeting. If you can master this one skill, you won't just be good at making money – more importantly, you will be good at keeping it.

The Basic Science of Budgeting

While having good Financial Health starts with earning money and keeping it, I like to add that it is more about how much you can *grow* what you keep. While saving and investing are not the same, learning how to save is the second step to anything that has to do with money after learning how to make it. Saving is probably one of the greatest tests of discipline, devotion, and will - all characteristics that are quintessential to sustaining a healthy relationship with money.

We've all heard the phrase about keeping up with the Jones' and as creatures of habit it is safe to say that as long as humans exist there will be a number of us who simply cannot resist the urge to spend money frivolously. Now I don't think this makes humans bad. If you work for your money you deserve to spend it how you want. The caveat, though, is you cannot say you "can't save". Maybe you don't care to eat Great Value FrootLoops so you buy your Kellogg's Fruit Loops which are about 20% more. Or maybe you have to have that BMW that costs $65,000 when the more reliable and less expensive Honda just doesn't do it for your 'lifestyle'. Maybe you just cannot live without the benefits of a big city so you opt out of the much more affordable suburban living.

Whatever it is, many of us choose our lifestyle for personal reasons and there's no problem with that so long as it is sustainable. The problem is, according to the data I shared earlier, for many people it is not. They don't notice the thousands of extra dollars they spend per year buying the on-brand products that are literally the same quality as the off-brand products (sometimes even better). They don't see that on top of the 60% higher retail price of buying that 'luxury' car versus a best value car is a hefty maintenance and gas bill over the lifetime of ownership in comparison. And it's easy to dismiss the fact that along with paying higher rent costs you're also more likely to go to bars and outside dining and engage in pricier activities while residing in the downtown of a big city instead of a suburb.

These are just some of the reasons why over half of America is stuck living paycheck to paycheck and why, unfortunately, many go broke the minute one major life event occurs. I hate to be the Debby-Downer here but I am passionate about this subject because I was one of those humans making my own mistakes of keeping up with Jones' and spending frivolously before realizing just how simple the remedy was. Unfortunately, I also know way too many who never acted on their knowledge of the same remedy and I would not want that to be you.

Now I will be the first to tell you that saving doesn't always feel or look sexy especially as you start out (which is why the sooner you start the better). Of course, the fancy car can be a head turner and probably looks better than the value car! I know we can all relate to how a new pair of kicks or clothes can make you walk with a bit more swag! And that high-rise condo downtown with floor to ceiling windows can have you walking around your apartment feeling like Ghost from Power! However, real power is having the self-control to keep a healthy relationship with money.

As you make money I challenge you to be a good steward of it and watch how it grows; and more importantly, watch how you grow. Before you know it you will be able to not just buy the lifestyle you desire, but afford it. There's a huge difference and it can easily be revealed by budgeting. Unfortunately, many don't realize this and fall victim to temporary flash paid for by long term stress and financial insecurity. That doesn't have to be you though, because you are being exposed to good Financial Health and developing the skills to control your Financial Health KPI!

Let's start by defining a budget – it's a tool that one uses to forecast, or logically predict, what their earnings and expenses would look like during a given period (e.g., for a week, a month, or a year). This is the foundation of any and every business, actually, and as someone who cares about their Financial Health you should be about your business. To create your own budget is much simpler than that of an actual business, though. All you need to think about is what you earn and what you spend. Here's how it works:

1st: Make a list of all the money you will bring in during a set period and label it "Earnings"

2nd: Make a list of all the money you will have to spend in the same period and label them "Expenses"

3rd: Add up your Earnings for the period and call it 'Total Earnings"

4th: Add up your Expenses for the same period and call it 'Total Expenses"

5th: Subtract your 'Total Expenses' from your Total Earnings

6th: What you're left with is your net profit or net loss (if the number is negative) for the period.

Using the scenario of the average person from earlier, let's model this now.

Earnings - Full Time Job Salary	$5,924
Expense - Rent	($1,724)
Expense - Water	($40)
Expense - Electricity/Wi-Fi	($120)
Expense - Cell Phone	($120)
Expense - Gas	($80)
Expense - Groceries	($700)
Expense – Car Note / Insurance	($640)
Expense – 'Live a Little' Fund	($500)
Retained Earnings (Earnings – Expenses)	**$2,000**

In this example you play the individual making $5,924 from your job. You rent a one-bedroom apartment in the city for $1,724 and your other living expenses needed to get by each month cost you an extra $1,700 for the month. Because you're human and honest with yourself you also know that all work and no play is bad for the mind, body, and spirit so you account for a moderate monthly limit of $500 to live a little. Counting this expense, you're now at a total of $3,924 in monthly expenses. If you spend only on those expenses and hit that earnings numbers your retained earnings or 'net income' equal $2,000 for the month. Now the major assumption behind this is that you will earn exactly that much and spend exactly that much for the upcoming month and that is what makes this list a budget!

Your budget is a breakdown of your flow of money based on *logical* and historic assumptions. For example, you can't just say you're going to make $10,000 next month if you don't actually have that incoming. That would make it a dream, not a budget. Now that we have defined this budget and made it real through this example, let's now simulate the act of budgeting. While the budget is a noun, budgeting is a verb – something that you actually do. The act of working to obtain that 'bottom line' number we call the 'retained earnings' or 'net income', is what budgeting looks like. It means that you are taking a disciplined approach to making what you need to make and only spending what you set out to spend in your budget. Simply put you always want to make at least what you said you would make and spend no more than what you said you would spend.

In business your budget is no more than a forecast, something that you logical predict will happen. The art of budgeting, though, means actually measuring your performance so let's expand that first example to see what I mean. At the end of the month you check your bank account and record within your budget the actual values for each of the categories you budgeted for and this is what you gathered:

Categories	Budget	Actuals	Difference
Full Time Job Salary	$5,924	$5,924	0
Rent	($1,724)	($1,724)	0
Water	($40)	($40)	0
Electricity/Wi-Fi	($120)	($140)	($20)
Cell Phone	($120)	($120)	0
Gas	($80)	($60)	$20
Groceries	($700)	($700)	0
Car Note/Insurance	($640)	($640)	0
'Live a Little' Fund	($500)	($400)	$100
Retained Earnings	**$2,000**	**$2,100**	**$100**

Look at that! You actually earned exactly how much you said you would earn because you have a consistent paycheck. Even better, you spent $200 less than you thought you would. Even though your electricity bill was $20 more than you expected based on your last bill and expected usage, your gas bill was $20 less than you expected. What's more is that you canceled plans with your friends to read The KPIs of Life one night and that actually saved you another $100 bringing your retained earnings to $2,100 for the month!

Good is when you hit the exact numbers that you budgeted to hit, but better is when you retain more earnings than you expected. You never want to be over budget, though. This tells you that you are not planning accordingly or that you lack self-control. Of course, things may come up and a miscellaneous or unexpected expense may have to get paid but this should not be the norm. Because life happens, let's breakdown what it means to advance your utility of money by covering a topic that will change your life – saving and investing.

A Little Caveat on Debt

Once you get ahold of money you must master the art and science of budgeting before you do anything else because without the discipline of budgeting it can become unnecessarily hard to do better things with your money. Once you have budgeting down, though, doing something with those retained earnings is a key next step. The best things to do with those earnings are save and invest them, with one real caveat – debt.

If you happen to have credit card or loan debt I highly recommend getting on a low interest payment plan, if you are not already, to tackle your debt. If you are able to pay it off completely, even better. Whatever you do, though, you must be diligent about staying out of high interest debt at all costs! Debt can be a real headache and severely handicap your ability to sustain good Financial Health. They call it the silent killer because it can also add a great deal of unnecessary stress to your life. So if that means incorporating your debt as an expense in your budget then you should do that so you can monitor the debt proactively and work at reducing it. One of the first things to do to control your debt is giving yourself a reality check and prioritizing debt over fun. That means, instead of allocating money for your "Live a Little" fund, you need to allocate that money to a 'Debt Elimination' bucket until your debt is paid off.

That being said, there is a such thing as good debt. Debt like student loan payments, mortgages, and business loans are not bad so long as you are not overleveraged or at risk of spending more on this debt than you make. If you have a large pile of credit card or personal loan debt, though, this is a bad position to be in and something that should be taken care of before you start saving and investing. Even if that means paying it off periodically, getting rid of bad debt is always above saving and investing so please take heed to this on your path to financial freedom and health. For the sake of example, let's add to our prior model a line item for 'good debt' to showcase how a budget including debt could look:

Categories	Budget	Actuals	Difference
Full Time Job Salary	$5,924	$5,924	0
Rent	($1,724)	($1,724)	0
Water	($40)	($40)	0
Electricity/Wi-Fi	($120)	($140)	($20)
Cell Phone	($120)	($120)	0
Gas	($80)	($60)	$20
Groceries	($700)	($700)	0
Car Note/Insurance	($640)	($640)	0
'Live a Little' Fund	($500)	($400)	$100
Student Loan Debt	($500)	($500)	0
Retained Earnings	**$1,500**	**$1,600**	**$100**

For most college graduates or business owners they have some debt from investing in something that enables them to now earn their salary. Again, this is good debt but it's still debt so we have to control it and eventually eliminate it over time so we must place it as an expense in our budget.

Saving & Investing

I think we all know that we have to save money to keep it, but the element of investing must be incorporated alongside saving to optimize the utility of our money. My rule of thumb is to save until you have six months of expenses saved up. I call this building a "Rainy Day Fund". I know that this may sound aggressive for some but no matter how long it takes, I know first-hand the freedom that this brings. You could go all in and just save every penny but I think dividing and conquering is a much better plan because time is a critical component to investing. So even if it is just five or ten dollars, I recommend investing as soon as possible to see the most benefit of compounded growth.

If you already have that Rainy Day Fund saved up, then you have a lot more room for growth! You can start allocating that portion of retained earnings to growing another pot of savings for something like opening up your own business, or investing more into the stock market or other asset classes. Maybe you want to own a home so you save for that; or maybe you want to reward yourself for staying disciplined so you want to save for a gift! So long as you have money allocated for a comfortable Rainy Day Fund AND an investment account, you can afford to look at other options.

Going back to the first control of having a healthy relationship with money, the financially fit person sees the utility of saving and investing as being just as necessary as paying rent. I like to see 'saving' as paying yourself to save yourself and I treat that practice as law because it stresses the foundational importance of preserving one's future. Investing is defined, *by Investopedia.com*, as "the deployment of capital towards projects or activities that are expected to generate a positive financial return over time". The key word is 'expected' here. By definition investing means putting your resource, in this case money, at some level of risk to be lost. I always want to be very clear about this. Luckily, some investments are more guaranteed than others, but we won't go there yet. Instead, let's continue with the example of what the *financially fit version of you* would do with your retained earnings on a month to month basis given the same earnings and expenses.

Categories	Budget	Actuals	Difference
Full Time Job Salary	$5,924	$5,924	0
Rent	($1,724)	($1,724)	0
Water	($40)	($40)	0
Electricity/Wi-Fi	($120)	($140)	($20)
Cell Phone	($120)	($120)	0
Gas	($80)	($60)	$20
Groceries	($700)	($700)	0
Car Note/Insurance	($640)	($640)	0
'Live a Little' Fund	($500)	($400)	$100
Student Loan Debt	($500)	($500)	0
Retained Earnings	**$1,500**	**$1,600**	**$100**
Savings (Rainy Day Fund)	($1000)	($1000)	0
Investing	($500)	($500)	0

Again, if you have a good amount of bad debt – high interest debt like credit cards and personal loans – you absolutely must incorporate and prioritize paying that off as part of your budget. However, in this case where you only have good debt – your student loan debt – you have already accounted for this as a monthly bill leaving you $1,600 in retained earnings. Instead of seeing this as "Live a Little More" money, it would be much more beneficial to your Financial Health KPI if you used that 25% of your income to grow and aid in your self-preservation. In other words, it would be more beneficial if you saved and invested those retained earnings.

I prioritize building a six-month expense savings account as the first option for what to do with retained earnings for a couple of reasons. First, there is no security in living pay check to pay check or practically month to month. As we learned from Maslow, security is necessary for achieving self-actualization. Saving specifically for six months of expenses provides you security in the long run because if you had to go without an income for some time or business gets slow at least you know your expenses are taken care of for at least six months. Hopefully that is substantially more than enough time to get back on your feet.

Second, freedom is a state of mind just as much as it is a state of being and the peace of mind that comes with having enough money to cover your needs for six months is a significant mark of financial freedom that you can only feel through personal experience. With enough money in your pocket to cover your needs in the event any unfortunate situation arises you can really start to see your net income month to month as money that you can 'afford to lose' and thus promote making more educated and calculated risks (i.e., investments). In fact, the sooner this happens the more aggressive your risks can be from the perspective that you likely have more time to recover in the event of failure.

One of the most significant differences in the mindset of the affluent versus that of the impoverished is the concept of survival. When you have to act out of survival it is much harder to have options and prioritize better over good let alone good for bad. When saving, think of investing as an option afforded to you once you have "money to lose" or money that would not be detrimental to you covering your needs in the short term. There are, of course, caveats to this. For example, if the benefit of making that investment far exceeds the cost of not making the investment like in the case of college, in which data proves that people with college degrees earn almost double in their lifetime compared to someone who did not go to college, making an investment in college well worth it on paper.

Nonetheless, saving enough to cover six months of expenses should provide not just a peace of mind but a bench mark of success for Financial Health KPI. Not to mention saving is the often-necessary practice of discipline for future financial goals as well and a safeguard from life's bad realities. Like we went over and like you can probably attest to depending on your age, things happen some times that are out of one's control. To remedy this, a best practice of mine is to always cut the excess first so in this case that means that the "Live a Little" bucket is what I cut first in the event I need money for something while I am trying to build my emergency fund, not my savings bucket.

At the end of the month if it turns out that I have estimated my budget perfectly then no harm, no foul. If things out of my control do come up and cost me, I have some room to handle it without any financial stresses. Again, having money is NOT everything but when you don't have it and NEED it... that becomes quite the conundrum so keep that in mind as you budget in real life.

Note: Once upon a time, putting your money under a mattress or hidden in the walls of your house was considered 'saving'. Then we evolved to something called 'the retail bank' – places like Wells Fargo and Bank of America, for example – here we could put our money in a safe where it was always accessible. There it would also get to grow like 1 cent for every $1000 you held there. Not bad, I guess, if the only other alternative was burying it in your backyard for it to mold. These days, though, many *banks allow you to hold your money in a high yield savings account with rates as high as 5%! That means just putting your $16,200 in their banks for a year would gain you $810! Now I'd say that's much better than the mattress play. For options you can do your own research but the best ones at the time of writing this in 2024 are SoFi and Ally Bank.*

I have talked about savings mostly so now we are ready to take that second step in the process of leveling up our budgeting which means we are ready to invest! Before we get into the math, let me share a story from personal experience to set the context. A few months before graduated from college I received a signing bonus of $15,000 from the company that I was about to start my full-time job with post-graduation (again, the benefit of high value skills are high value earnings). Now after taxes this was only about $10,000 but at the time it was the most money I had ever received in one lump sum.

At that moment the light bulb clicked and instead of spending it on the latest fashion or wasting it frivolously I vowed to do well with this money so, feeling like I had just won the lottery and didn't want anyone to know, I researched "what to do with money" (you probably see a trend with me at this point). As you could imagine I found endless articles on Google but what I landed on was *investing*. Up until that point I had not learned much about investing. As an Industrial Engineer and Physics double major I learned a lot of stuff but in terms of numbers, I only took ambiguous math classes like Linear Algebra and Differential Equations, nothing practical or useful like Business Finance or Accounting. So while I had heard the term 'investing' before from peers and exposure I didn't know how to invest nor did I think that it was any more useful than giving money to a baby. Up until that point I had been laser focused on just finding out how to make money.

Kids who majored in Business or who had parents/peers that talked to them about finances had that advantage over me - they were exposed to finance in this way earlier. Even though I had what I thought was a great privilege of obtaining knowledge from my mom, parents in high school, and peers I constantly learned how much I was only scratching the surface. What I realized in that night of learning about investing through rabbit holes on Google and YouTube is that I was worried about the wrong thing all these years. Making money isn't the most valuable thing, knowing how to make it work for you is.

From that point on my relationship with money changed. I was no longer focused on making money and spending it on what I wanted; I was now focused on making money and growing it how I wanted! That one night put all those years in pursuit of making money to the backseat of finding ways to grow it and if you only take that one perspective from this chapter, that alone would be good enough. If you want to know if you have a good mindset on money ask yourself 'do I look for ways to grow the money I have?' Focusing on how to grow my money changed my life but it wasn't until I got good at budgeting that I realized that it could.

Through budgeting you can see that if you're spending more than you make then you're not making money at all really and if you don't know what you're spending each month you're setting yourself up for failure big time. So let's jump back into our Financially Fit self and track how they would invest their money after allocating $1,000 of their retained earnings into saving. Instead of spending the extra $500 you've saved by the end of the month you could add to your savings, but investing would be the smarter move to make for your overall Financial Health KPI and I'll tell you why in what follows.

I shared my story of coming into investing because I wanted to share how natural it is to be totally ignorant to something and how easy it is to become knowledgeable. While there are many options for where to invest this $500 I would start by looking into if my salaried job offers a '401K Plan'. If you are not familiar with a 401K plan it is a retirement plan that many employers provide where said employer takes money from your paycheck and invests it in a 401K Plan provider, like Vanguard or Fidelity, for you. 401Ks are a safe entry point into the often volatile but equally rewarding stock market. 401Ks invest your money into what are called Exchange Traded Funds (or ETFs for short) which is a collection of stocks packaged into one 'security' allowing you to invest in fractions of a share of multiple stocks. While the upside of ETFs is nowhere near that of a singular stock, the positive about that is that the downside is nowhere near as bad as a singular stock either. Meaning, individual stocks can jump 10% or more in a day but they can also fall by 10% in price. On the other hand, ETFs will probably never see a 10% increase in price but they certainly won't see a 10% decrease overnight either. And even though you can invest in ETFs on your own, the reason why I would start investing in a 401K if you can is because of three primary benefits:

1st: It's a tax benefit. Every year the IRS sets a limit on how much an individual can invest into their 401K plan. In 2024 it was $23,000 so if you earned a $71,000 salary you would be able to reduce your tax liability significantly by simply investing in your future! Meaning instead of paying the taxes on $71,000 you would only pay taxes on $48,000. If this is a new concept to you, just multiply $71,000 times 22% - the tax rate in 2024 for someone making $71,000. Now multiply that same 22% by $48,000. The difference is a savings of just over $5,000 so in essence you'd be investing $6,000 and saving $5,000 on taxes (if you were to max out your 401k investment). That's what separates investing in a 401K from investing in the stock market – investing in the stock market does not save you money on taxes. In fact, you pay what is called "capital gains" taxes on any profits made.

2nd: This reason is not exactly guaranteed but if you have the option it's one of the only legal ways to obtain free money in this country. It is what is known as a 'company match' program. In essence a match program is where an employer matches your contributions into a 401K Plan for a specific percentage of your investment up to a certain percentage of your salary (generally, less than 10%). For example, if you have a $60,000 salary and your employer matches you .50 cent for every dollar you contribute up to 6% of your salary what that means is that they would contribute 6% of $60,000 multiplied by .5 or $1,800. That's $1,800 of their money that they pay into your 401K account. So on top of the tax savings your earn by investing in a 401K you also earn free money if your employer offers the match. Now not all companies offer this 'match' but many do so look for them. It's something that you can inquire about with your company at any time or when you are interviewing. Even if your company does not offer a match program the first benefit and the next are still great reasons to start your investing journey by investing in a 401K.

3rd: Probably more important than the monetary value itself, a 401K possess another benefit that I believe is underappreciated and that is the protection of your investment. And by protection, I mean from yourself. One of the often talked about downsides of a 401k is the fact that you have to pay taxes on any money you pull out of it before you turn 65. In fact, many banks even charge you a flat fee for pulling out of it. While there is merit in this concern, if you are truly investing this can be the best thing that can be done for you because it keeps you from getting in the way of the phenomenon of compounding. The more you put into a 401K Plan the more it will grow over time because the interest just keeps compounding on itself. Same as investing in individual stocks but 401Ks provide extra layers of guardrails to keep your money working for you and prevent you from interrupting that work. In investing 1+1 doesn't always equal 2. Sometime 1+1 equals 100 if given enough time!

If you need an extra boost of encouragement, consider the fact that if you manage to give yourself two years to stick to your plan and in year three nothing changes in terms of your income and base expenses, that $1,500 of retained earnings can now be completely utilized for further investing while you have a comfortable nest egg of savings and you have started investing for your future. So focus on the delayed gratification of setting yourself up to be in a supreme financial situation in the future as you stay committed to the discipline of sticking to your budget. A year or two of staying committed to becoming Financially Healthy can set you up for a lifetime of prosperity and save you from a life of stress.

By building a budget – truly putting pen to paper or fingers to keyboard – you are keeping yourself honest about what you have and what you need. This practice, consistently, was truly the game changer for me because it allowed me to analyze my life in a measurable way. It's not just about the earnings and expenses, it's also about the eye-opening realization of where your money goes that is of benefit to most. Seeing is believing, they say, and with budgeting this is certainly true because the consciousness and awareness gained through studying your financial situation at this forensic level is all the catalyst one should need to get real about their finances and make improvements where needed.

A Deeper Look Into Investing:

Investing, by nature, is a risky act but as the popular saying goes, "high risk, high reward!" Investing doesn't just have to be in the stock market. You can invest in real estate in various forms from single-family housing to REITs (which work like ETFs except with real estate assets instead of shares of companies). You can invest in art, the crypto market, your own business, and more. By far the best investment you can make, though, is an investment in yourself. All this requires is patient and persistent curiosity to grow. In the same way that investing your money unleashes the powers of compounding so does investing in getting better at something everyday. When you are constantly investing in ways to become better the effects compound over time and you will be able to look back and see substantial growth.

Start by learning one thing per day; work your way up to having conversations about it; figure out ways to meet new people to discuss what you are learning. The key to investing is to build a growth mindset! Towards both yourself and your finances in this case. As you give that practice your honest effort you will learn and make mistakes but that is only part of the journey. Remember that saying 'time in the market is better than timing the market' – it works for yourself as well. The sooner you can get started on the journey of investing in yourself the better.

From a more material perspective, when I speak of investing I do mean literally putting your money in vehicles that will grow faster and larger than it would if you just leave it in a bank. As I mentioned earlier, in this day and age there is a such thing as high-yield savings accounts but I still do not consider that investing. Consider this – here are the 5 year returns of investing in 5 popular companies' stock (from 2019-2024):

- Coca-Cola = 27%
- Netflix = 97%
- Walmart = 126%
- Facebook = 183%
- Apple = 331%

While putting your money in a high-yield savings account that gains 4% per year is certainly better than putting it in a traditional bank account that gains practically nothing, clearly it's not the same as investing.

Investing does not have to be hard but there is an inherent risk involved in the sport by nature. I'll break it down to you like this to explain why: investing is a trade-off that you believe to be of mutual benefit and risk. In other words there's an emotional component – something has to give you a *feeling* that what you're investing in is worth it because of the payoff. You may have heard about it, or googled it, or know someone who served as proof. Whatever it is it has to feel like the right decision to you. The science of it is that most, if not all, *sound* investments have plenty of data to back them up.

The easiest way to make sound investments for most is through the stock market. There is endless amounts of data online to validate whatever gut feeling you have about investing in a company. The barrier to entry is also non-existent. All you have to do is open up a brokerage account and connect it to whatever checking account you own and you are off to the races on your investing journey. I certainly understand how intimidating investing can seem if you have never done it before but the quicker you get started the quicker you will realize how simple it is and how profitable it can be for you.

My personal preference is to practice something called dollar cost averaging when it comes to investing. Dollar cost averaging is the practice and discipline of investing the same amount of money into a particular stock or portfolio of stocks at a consistent frequency. There are many good reasons why I believe in this practice but here are the most important ones:

- It allows you to avoid the risk of investing a large amount at a market peak. This helps mitigate the impact of short-term market fluctuations and reduces the risk associated with trying to time the market
- Since you're buying at various prices, you also average out the cost of your investments. When prices are high, you buy fewer shares, and when prices are low, you buy more. This can result in a lower average cost per share over time.
- Investing regularly means your money can start compounding sooner. Even small, consistent investments can grow significantly over time due to the power of compounding.
- Dollar cost averaging helps you stick to a plan without being swayed by market volatility or emotional reactions. This can prevent impulsive decisions that might lead to buying high and selling low.

The reality of the stock market is that prices fluctuate and over the lifetime of a stock the price will almost always rise (that's why you invest!). One day Coca-Cola is worth $50 per share, the next it can be worth $55 per share. At the time of writing this the share price is actually just under $70.

By dollar cost averaging you protect yourself from ever buying high and selling low which is opposite of the goal of investing. You always want to buy an asset for as little as you can and sell it for higher but this requires not just time in the market to watch your investment grow but also time in the market to know what a low price is versus a high price. If you see that a promising stock is $50 and you bought it a month ago for $55 you will see that $5 decrease as a sale and not a permanent drop. By buying the stock at the new price of $50 you have decreased the average price that you pay for the stock which means when you eventually sell it for a higher price you will have a larger return.

Overall, dollar-cost averaging is a practical strategy that can help manage investment risks and foster a steady growth trajectory over time. So long as you see investing as a long-term play (e.g., for more than just a few years) then you will almost inevitably see positive returns on your investments with this strategy. As mentioned before, the stock market isn't the only way to invest but I do believe that it is the most accessible for most because you can buy stocks for as little as pennies. To reiterate, though, the earlier you start the more promising it will be. And just like investing in yourself, the more time and intention you put into it the better off you will be so long as you do not lose patience and discipline because all great things take time.

The Purpose of Money

So you understand that money's utility is that it can be saved, spent, and invested; you understand that acquiring money means acquiring skills that pay; and you know about monitoring your income and spending habits by way of budgeting. Now what? There's no overnight difference, no week-to-week difference, maybe not even a month-to-month difference. Your life hasn't changed much if at all since you started this chapter, so what is the point? To that I say – that's OK! Stick with it.

In managing your Financial Health KPI by developing a healthy relationship with money, learning high-value skills, and budgeting consistently you should also be understanding what the purpose of obtaining and keeping money is for you. Morgan Housel, the author of the legendary book The Psychology of Money, posed a thought in that book that was transformative to me. He said, "most people don't want a million dollars, they want to spend a million dollars". That made me critically think about my relationship with money and I share it with you in hopes that those words allow you the same moment of reflection.

Before I read those words I didn't really focus on money from a place of purpose. I just knew that I wanted money to buy things that I or my loved ones did not have. After constant reflection and time spent growing, my values changed. I began to care less about what I could buy and more about what I could do, who I could help, and what I could build for my future even when I am no longer on this Earth. These desires became my purpose which made it easier for me to save money for investing purposes instead of saving to buy a good that did not appreciate in time. Knowing that I wanted to have money for my future family made it easier to turn down spending money on overpriced drinks at a club every weekend which allowed me to spend time developing skills and spending quality time in other, less taxing, ways.

When you live with purpose you are empowered to persevere. So start with committing to the goal of taking a disciplined approach to developing your Financial Health KPI but spend time reflecting on why you want to develop this KPI. In time you will come to realize for yourself that the answer to that question is your purpose and with that purpose it should become easier for you to say no to anything to that does not help serve that purpose for you.

I would like to tell you that your purpose for money should be bigger than just obtaining things, but I am not here to tell you what to do with your money. I have my perspective but what I care about is that you understand what it takes to become financially fit, and more importantly, that you can sustain that state. That is the ultimate purpose and measure of success for any of your KPIs – being able to sustain the good health of these performance indicators.

So as long as you understand how to meet and improve your Financial Health KPI through time, I am satisfied enough with that and would like to leave it up to you to determine what purpose you have for obtaining money. If you can maintain the discipline that it requires to ensure this KPI stays in a good state I have faith that you can and will determine for yourself what purpose you have for your money. Tying back to Maslow's theory, sustaining Financial Health actually fits in every category on your way to self-actualization by virtue of reality because even those basic physiological needs require money, and as we discussed, failure to manage your money can result in poor circumstance but you are more than capable of being better than that.

Lastly, I cannot stress enough how much time plays a factor in all of our KPIs. Gaining exposure, developing valuable skills, maintaining a budget, saving, and investing all require time and intentional effort which means that you cannot grow weary or impatient with the process. While this can seem easier said than done you must see this as a tradeoff. You either put in the effort now so that the future is significantly easier or you put off doing the work now and make for a more challenging life later. That is the truth of the matter and that is why purpose plays such a big part in the equation.

KPI 3: Mental & Emotional Health

Disclaimer:
I am not a psychologist nor certified therapist nor am I an expert on mental and emotional health for all humans; I am only an expert on myself. Even still, I won't say that I am an expert on articulating my mental and emotional health. In fact, I grew up in a world where mental health and emotional health weren't even part of my community's lexicon. Sometimes I look back over my life and I feel thankful that I wasn't introduced to these good concepts because growing up brought some catastrophically bad days. Some of the things that I and my family members have endured and witnessed other human beings do would cause any sane person to lose themselves. In those times of crises all we knew to do was move forward the best way we knew how, nevermind if it was healthy or not. I sometimes think if I knew who to turn to and how to articulate the pain and traumas to another human then I would not have been able to lean so fully on God and test His ability to provide me what I needed in my times of despair.

I cannot explain how I persevered all of the things I have preserved; only that I know I had God with me. I think if we all look back over some of the lows in our lives we could say the same. For what I can explain, though, what follows is my best attempt to provide something to help us all build a strong Mental & Emotional Health KPI. This one chapter is by no means meant to serve as a solution to all of life's problems. I simply hope to share pieces of my life that I believe most can relate to and observations made from moments of reflection.

I am thankful that I eventually learned to value this aspect of life. Like I do with most things, I spent significant time examining and exploring well researched methods to enhance my Mental & Emotional Health KPI as well as things I found intrinsic. If you ever need assistance with your mental and emotional health I hope my vulnerability gives you the same permission to be vulnerable and get whatever help you need. I wish anyone well who is battling with things unseen and I pray that my thoughts here provide a safe place of assistance.

A Tough Subject

So far, I've made the case – alongside Maslow's Hierarchy of Needs – that achieving lasting success begins with two foundational pillars: Physical Health and Financial Health. If you can sustain both, I believe you're far more likely to experience consistent progress and peak moments of fulfillment. After all, it's a simple truth: you need money to live well, and you need a healthy body to live long.

I've offered both philosophical context and practical tools to help you measure and maintain these areas. But what lies ahead is perhaps the most nuanced KPI of all – Mental and Emotional Health. Unlike the external benchmarks of money or physical strength, this domain is invisible, deeply personal, and profoundly influential. It's the most primitive aspect of who we are, yet one of the most impossible to fit us all the same. On the same note, without tending to this KPI, all other KPIs risk falling apart.

This subject is tricky and for good reason, controversial, because of the subjective nature of it. I can point you to a thousand think pieces on how to manage your mental and emotional health. I can share a hundred stories of how someone with a great upbringing went on to be a complete disaster of a human being and I can give you stories of people who underwent the most atrocious of traumas yet went on to live successful and impactful lives. I can break down ways in which coming from poverty puts one's mental and emotional health at greater risk than coming from affluence and I can also break down how it can breed advantages. The thing is, though, none of that matters because effective mental and emotional health development is only effective if it works for you.

If you eat a healthy diet and work out consistently, granted you have no chronic or impairing health conditions, you can control your Physical Health KPI. If you gain valuable skills to earn more than you spend and master financially fit budgeting you will control your Financial Health KPI. With Mental and Emotional Health, there's a lot to it that no one person can possibly know for all.

Mental and Emotional Health contributes to all of our other KPIs. A good Mental and Emotional Health KPI is not just the absence of mental disorders or being in complete control of your emotions at all times. It encompasses a positive sense of well-being and the ability to enjoy life while on Earth. Conversely, a poor Mental and Emotional Health KPI can negatively affect a person's thoughts, feelings, and behavior leading to difficulties in functioning and impairing their quality of life be it internal or external. With this you can see why this subject is so, if not the most, complex yet important to reaching self-actualization or a state of fulfillment in life.

I am no doctor of any sort nor do I have extensive scholastic knowledge of all facets of Mental and Emotional Health but I do have my lived experiences, which are unique to me, but may resonate on some level with you and others. To that end, like the preceding chapter, the direction of this chapter will be one of transparency and my own perspective on Mental and Emotional Health through those experiences as it relates to achieving fulfillment.

Again, I am not a doctor. I have never been diagnosed with any disorders professionally nor have I ever sought it out so I cannot speak personally on diagnosed disorders. I do acknowledge that mental illnesses are real and believe that if you think you have a disorder then you should reach out to a medical professional. I care about the people of our world reaching self-actualization and without good Mental and Emotional Health I don't believe self-actualization can ever really exist. For what good is beauty if it cannot be beholden? For what is love if it can't be felt? In the same way, what good is it to achieve everything that looks good on the outside when you are suffering from within?

As I shared at the start of this book, I was not born into much but I was blessed with a mother who made a way every day. Through her own devising she took us out of the southside of Chicago and into the suburbs of Dallas. When we found ourselves in a place fiscally out of what came to be our norm, she worked her way to providing even more than what we were used to. If you go by statistics from the time I was born, it is more probable that I would have been dead or in jail than it is that I would have written this book. As a black man born out of wedlock to teen parents in Chicago's inner city it was much more likely that I would have dropped out of high school than it is that I would have graduated college with two STEM degrees. Now that isn't to say that living through these conditions are guarantees of failure but the data does correlate much of my early life scenarios to failure.

I failed classes yet I still went on to build a career in corporate America working for the largest retail bank in America, one of the best investment banks in the world, and two of the largest consulting firms in the world. I didn't achieve my childhood dream of going to the NFL but I still managed to live out my dreams of traveling the world, having traveled to over 50 countries and counting! I have been arrested for marijuana possession yet I still play an active role in making positive impacts to my community having raised thousands of dollars to help aspiring students attend the same college where I was arrested. I showed up to client meetings with CEOs less than 24 hours after attending the funerals of some of my closest loved ones. The very first day of my professional career was the day after I held my mother before she went to prison. None of this is stated to field pity or glorify struggle, and it should not be used as a measuring post for what life should look like. What I am sharing are the many facets of a 'regular' life that can have varying impacts on our Mental and Emotional Health.

I would imagine that it isn't hard to categorize the positive and negative experiences I just mentioned but if you asked me, I would tell you with all sincerity that the culmination of those experiences as a whole were beneficial to me building a strong Mental & Emotional Health KPI and reaching my own state of self-actualization. Through the highs and lows of life I have managed to stay level headed and maintain control of my Mental and Emotional Health through my own controls related to this subject and this chapter takes you on a personal journey of my own experiences of realizing, developing, and utilizing these controls. But these aren't just mine. After talking to strangers and people close to me about the subject I also saw these as trends that I consider to be foundational:

THE KPIS OF LIFE

1. Have a source of empowerment
2. Have a fighting spirit
3. Mind your thoughts
4. Have an attitude of gratitude
5. Just keep pushing

It took me about six months to write this book initially and most of that time I spent monitoring my own Mental and Emotional Health and studying the subject. Strangers, loved ones, generative AI and experts alike all agreed that Mental and Emotional Health go hand in hand. Sometimes our emotional state drives our mental; sometimes it's the other way around; and sometimes it's external forces alone that impact both. I do not know what works for everyone but what I want to suggest is that if we can focus more on controlling our minds, then our emotions will be much easier to control. Growing up I experienced trauma, love, safety, and fear as often as I experienced each of the yearly seasons. Some warmer than others and some colder, but all rotational nevertheless. Over time I believe I built mental fortitude that started to dictate not *what* I felt, necessarily, but *how* I felt it and without always knowing it I attribute that to those controls.

Before I Knew Better

I was just born into this world, not born with knowledge of it. Where I'm from in Chicago kids had a place but were still talked to as adults. This meant that cursing wasn't a violent response rather just a regular part of the vernacular and so was being made fun of. Fighting was a sport and you had to be skilled or suffer the consequences at time of any dispute. Nutrition consisted of anything that you could find at the corner store and the food label was no better than the terms and condition we all claim to read before clicking "Agree" on a website. The subject of mental health was so taboo that going to a therapist was seen as no different that seeing a shrink. Everyone was the product of a broken home or family to some extent and fathers were either dead or deadbeats. This was the life that I knew and grew up accustomed to.

After what feels like only a summer, life changed. I went from this world where everyone was the same shade of color and had the same vernacular to a world where it was the total opposite. School was now full of kids from all over the world; we went to grocery stores instead of corner stores; and all we had was mom at home. This was what it looked like moving from 'the hood' of Chicago to a military base town in Killeen, TX. After that year we moved just about every year. If it wasn't to a new state it was at least to a new city or part of town. While that may seem uncomfortable for some, I can't say that bothered me much – it was one of those 'it is what it is' realities because by the time I could understand the moving it was all that I had known. Besides, I never had a choice so I was quite literally going with the flow.

I was a quiet kid but an observant one so all of these moves allowed me a different perspective of life and though I did not say much, I experienced everything as a bystander. My mom was young and hip so we always looked 'fresh', as she would say, and she took us everywhere she went – from the nail salon to the mall; from haircuts to church. She had old ways, though. We were like her little toy soldiers – disciplined and well-mannered or else we were liable to get a chunk of skin pinched out of us by her vice like grip. You knew better than to be the reason a teacher called home because of conduct or let her find out at the end of the quarter that you got poor grades… the kinds of whippings she would give can only be defined as corporal punishment.

Both of my siblings and I felt this wrath and it was anxiety inducing, but how I grew up no one spoke of things like anxiety. No matter which one of us was being stripped to our bare skin and whipped with belts or extension cords, all of us walked on egg shells for days for fear of *getting in the way* and causing our lieutenant to get mad. It didn't take me too many whippings to vow that I was going to stay out of trouble. Paying attention in class was a lot easier knowing that if it got back to my mom that I was doing something wrong that she would spend what felt like the whole night making tic tac toe boards across my backside with whatever she could get ahold of.

Don't get me wrong now, life was exceedingly good for us minus a few really traumatic outliers. I knew this then and even now but it took years before I could see that the bad had critical effects on my Mental & Emotional Health KPI. My timid and quiet nature put me in a position to just observe and form deep empath behaviors that showed up as insecurities. I started to feel a particular feeling when there was tension around. I could feel when others were sad to the point where I became sad. It's like if someone I knew was hurt I felt hurt, too. I didn't speak much out of fear of saying the wrong thing and suffering humiliation from being made fun of. At that age I didn't know what any of this meant or how to truly process the feelings but I did learn ways to mitigate these reactive feelings and eventually mitigate the impact they had on my mind and behaviors.

Norming and Forming

We moved to Memphis, TN right before I began 1st grade. When a family tragedy struck the summer before I began middle school life felt like it had hit it's lowest point; and while I had no control or input over what was going on, I felt like I had personally failed and that everything was my fault. I felt so conflicted during this time period because everything I had known about life up until that point had suddenly felt wrong and left me in a state of confusion and deep fear. My brother and I were sent to stay with my mom's childhood best friend in the suburbs of Chicago as a means to protect us from the tragedy. From the time my brother and I left Memphis until weeks into our stay in Chicago I stayed awake letting anger fill my heart.

At our family friend's house it was just like what we had left; it was a nice house with a couple of nice cars in a good neighborhood but the house felt tense just like ours. Without consciously trying to I alienated myself. I knew that due to the circumstances that our altruistic hosts would leave me be when I said I didn't feel like talking so I spent most of my nights that summer deep in my thoughts and growing more emotional. In this state I was overwhelmed with a helpless feeling which made me frustrated and irritable to the point where I didn't even want to speak to my little brother who was impacted just as I was, if not worse.

One day I decided to turn on the Playstation that was in the room that I was staying in and spent hours playing NFL Streetz. Before I knew it that is all that I wanted to do. It was the only thing that allowed me to escape where my mind, body, and spirit was. A few days later I found a Bible in one of the drawers and I was compelled to read it. I had heard a million Bible scriptures by this point in life having been a part of a strict Christian family. To me, the Bible wasn't like the Guinness Books of World Record that I would buy and study every year nor was it something I would pick up from the Scholastic Book Fair at school. I saw it as sacred and intimidating but for some reason on this day I decided to start it from scratch.

For the rest of that summer I spent all day reading the Bible and all night playing Playstation. I read the stories of the seven days that it took God to form the world as we know it and the ones of Adam and Eve's experience with the bliss of knowledge. My fear of God grew as I read of the Commandments and sacrifices of animals and people that God demanded of Noah and Abraham.

I spent car rides obsessively reflecting on how someone so omnipotent would let so much bad happen and found parallels in how God treated us with how I was raised. I eventually found comfort in stories like that of Joseph who was abandoned by his family yet still found glory. Some chapters made me cry and some gave me conflicting feelings like the story of Job and how he was stripped of his riches and deprived of everything good he had worked for only to be redeemed by God much later.

As I read of God's grace and mercy; the miracles of Jesus, His death, and how Revelations says the world will be when God returns, I recall being filled with mixed emotions about everything that I knew of life. During my elementary years in Memphis we spent a lot of time in church so I was quite familiar with "the word", but reading the Bible from front to back only left me in this crazy paradox I felt that I was living in. One which I could only escape when I was making cartoon players throw and catch fire blazed footballs on the Playstation. Most often, though, the video games only filled a void temporarily. Not before long I would feel the urge to read more. The stories made this God character to be so methodical and downright mean but also poetic in favor and almighty enough to never count out. It was like reading the Greek myths of their gods except I was born into a belief that these stories weren't myths.

This juggernaut I was going through was the beginning of how my Mental & Emotional Health KPI began to norm and form. In retrospect it was one of the broadest periods of growth and maturation for me. I had more questions than answers and no one to talk to for that summer. For an 11-year-old kid, reading the Bible was as traumatic as anything I had actually experienced but equally revitalizing in ways that I only began to see that summer. I was full of fear of what was to come given our circumstances but I eventually found solace in learning about God on my own.

The way I began to view the world during that time period awakened a new sense of self for me in retrospect. Songs that I would hear in church became more than just rhyme schemes to make people clap their hands. In every song I began to recognize a particular scripture.

'they that wait, on the Lord, shall renew their strengths.
They will mount up on....'
Or
'Noooo weapon... formed against me... shall prosper'

Slowly but surely I drew more and more parallels to life and the Bible and through my other past time of playing NFL Streetz I also drew parallels. For that entire summer I was either reading my bible or playing that video game. What playing NFL Streetz did for me was provide a conduit through which I could express myself. As I played the game more I found a desire to play the sport when, at one point earlier in life, I thought that it was the most terrifying thing to do. Between football and the Bible, for the first time, I had decisively discovered something in life that compelled me to the point of overriding other emotions. When I was playing that game or reading my Bible I left this world and became consumed in the world within that screen or within those scriptures and everything was alright.

By the time my mother and sister arrived in that Chicago suburb to pick up my brother and I the car was already packed up and without any advance notice I found out in transit that we were moving to Georgia. Unprepared, on that 11-hour road trip all I had was one book – the Phantom and the Tollbooth - which I had read a dozen times at that point and a CD player. Neither of which I had touched that summer.

During our years in Memphis the only time I heard anything other than gospel was when I spent the night at my one friend's house or if we were watching Showtime at the Apollo as a family.

In that household, my stepdad at the time made listening to anything but gospel feel like a sin so the only CDs we owned were gospel. During this trip my mom was all of a sudden listening to Monica, Brandy, and Mary J. Blige. At some point along our journey we stopped by a record store and she asked if I wanted to buy a CD for my player. Up until this point in life my mom also never let us make our own decisions. Anything from what we wore to what we ate to where we went, she was the sole decision maker, so at this moment I was in a state of paralysis almost completely unaware of what was going on.

I remember standing there paused and the first CD that I noticed was *College Dropout* by Kanye West. Looking back it makes a lot more sense why that particular album popped out. Having spent the last few months in Chicago, from which he was a native, I heard his song 'All Falls Down' just about every time a radio was on so it was likely subconsciously stuck in my brain. When I brought the album to my mom she looked at it front and back and said 'you sure you want this one?'. Again, dumbfounded by this rare request and still that timid little boy by nature, I just looked at her and slightly nodded.

When I popped that CD into my CD player it's like my whole life had changed in that one hour and a half it took for the album to play completely through. At the tender age of 11 every word he rapped spoke to me as if we were friends. As if he grew up in my house. Gospel was like the voice of my church but this album was like the voice of my home and of my upbringing. From the ad libbed interludes, the gospel-like melodies, to the ways he described life through rhymes, it all resonated with me as familiar. By the fourth rotation of the album I pretty much had the whole thing memorized and the lyrics became as real to me as the Bible. They made me grow up on that journey and gave me a newfound braveness as I visualized yet another new reality, but this time not just in a new school but in a whole new state again.

A Moment for Goliath

Life was different for us that first year. It was just a mama bear and her three cubs again, this time in a two-bedroom apartment north of Atlanta in a city called Duluth. No big house with a backyard and our own basketball goal, no cousins or grandparents around, and no male figure around. My mom was a single mother for the first time that I could really comprehend and feel the impact of. In Memphis we were accustomed to her taking us to school and picking us up everyday. As the sole provider for herself and her kids she now worked a job that required her to be at the office by 8 AM. Because we were young, she still had to wake us up so she would take us to school and we would ride the bus back.

At my school, kids whose parents had to work early could get dropped off before school opened to wait for it to start so my sister and I were those kids. Along with us was a kid that always made fun of me and would always push me around any time he got within arm's reach. I was never the biggest kid but back then I was especially frail with buck teeth and bifocals. Add to the fact that I was still timid and shy and it was really just Darwinism that I was experiencing. Not to mention the only person you would ever catch me with was this Jimmy Neutron looking white kid who had an obsession with football and Eminem. When I say obsessed I mean his parents let him come to school wearing a black bandana under a hat cocked to the side and at any given moment if we were together he was bound to bust out an Eminem rap with the same energy as Marshall Mathers himself.

Between classes is about the only time I had to deal with my bully and the five minutes or so after school at the bus line before my sister would get there. He never bothered me when my sister was around but on one particular day all factors in life conspired to make it a bad day for me. My friend James was out sick and my bully finally got his day to find me fully vulnerable.

When first period passed and I made my way to music class he spotted me walking by myself, and like a thief in the night he walked past me snatching my backpack and as the momentum pulled me forward he slipped his foot out to trip me. With the burn on my knee stinging and my big ass bifocals knocked halfway across the hallway I get up wobbling and as I reached to push him back he pulled me forward and tripped me again with me falling on the same knee. In the instant between me being over on my knees and me sitting upright against the lockers all the students filled the hallways. I remember sitting there with the defeat coming not so much from the battle I had just lost but from the fact that I couldn't see well enough to find where my glasses were. It took some time but I finally found them and, of course, they had been completely broken from the stampede of students storming the halls. For the rest of the day I was walking around limping, clothes looking worn and tired, and with lop sided bifocals held together with tape. It was the middle school equivalent of wearing the scarlet letter. Utter embarrassment.

I went through each period radiating with embarrassment and growing fear with every class change that I may have another interaction with my bully. During lunch I had my head on a swivel as I passed through the line as fast as I could. I didn't see any sign of him as I went from being in the back of the line to being at the Plexiglas window where I would receive my tray of food. I was one of those kids that had reduced lunch so I had to punch a number in on a keypad so that the lunch lady could identify me as such even though I had walked through her line 5 days a week for 2 months. For some reason, the lunch lady decided today was the day she would stall me in line.

"I know yo mama ain't send you to school looking like this, boy", she proclaimed

"I fell running outside" I responded swiftly

The look on her face told me she knew that I was lying. She just looked me up and down shook her head. Ashamed and guilty I dropped my head and moved past her as quickly as I could. The second I lifted my head and turned to walk out there he was like the grim reaper himself. He jerked at me and I jumped causing my food to fly everywhere. I had met Goliath before David on this day and Goliath put me to shame.

The middle school lunch room was like Showtime at the Apollo. Anything that went down there was the talk of the day and you were on stage to either get cheers or, as would most often be the case, get clowned by the audience. You didn't have to be there to know the goofball that dropped his food. The sheer sound of it was enough to cause chaos in a room full of middle schoolers and the mess that it made on all of my clothes was just the Scarlet Letter I needed to top off a humiliating day.

I just wanted the day to be over; hell, maybe even life at that point. It was just a horrible day to be alive in my head. No Kanye West song, no football game, no Bible verse provided me any comfort, and I had no one to turn to. That shell I had built around my aura hardened in that moment and I was stricken with equal parts fear, anxiety, and embarrassment. For the rest of the day I went to the rest of my classes much after the bell rang because I spent a few minutes hiding from the cause of my affliction. What I couldn't escape, though, was the after-school bus line. My sister was in 8th grade and because she was the talkative one with friends she always arrived at the bus stop a few minutes late with the other cool kids.

After the day that I had I again waited in my class as long as I could. As I walked to the bus stop I walked softly looking around for the bully and hoping to buy more time for my sister to come. I got outside a few minutes later than I normally did but waited by the door as to not show my face to the public out of fear of Goliath. The problem is he had been looking for me and like a shark when it smells blood, he sensed the pheromones of fear and found me cornered between a wall and a door. I surrendered my hands up as a white flag indicating that I didn't want any problems but he insisted.

He attempted to snatch my backpack as both straps were on my shoulder and as we wrestled he got stronger, pulling at my clothes and again knocking my glasses from my face. I was able to yield some momentum as he had me crouched so I lifted myself to push him away and before I could brace myself his right fist kissed me perfectly on my left eye. I sat there crying as my eye throbbed and the only positive to the situation was that only me, him, and some of his buddies saw what had happened. By the time my sister arrived to the scene the tears of hurt had turned into tears of anger and my head was buried into my knees as my arms held them together.

Word must had gotten around to my sister that I had a bully because when she found me she just yelled,

"did that boy do this to you?"

I looked up at her and just began to sob in fury.

"Don't worry, we got something for him" she exclaimed.

A Moment for David

My sister was a bit of a tomboy and as far as I knew she was the one person that I knew who could fight. Though we grew up in the same household life dealt her a harsher hand so she had a feistiness to her that was remnant of our mother's. She helped me get up and holding my hand pulled me to the bus stop in hopes of running into my bully but he had already left on his bus.

That night when I got home my mom saw my condition and the way she was raised was if you lost a fight, you had to go back for a supervised rematch. So, like any mom would, she began interrogating me and my sister on what happened and where I would be able to see this boy again. I didn't have to say a word because my sister explained everything as if she was there for everything. She told her how she heard about a sixth grader getting into a fight in the hallway; how everyone was talking about the kid who got pushed at lunch and spilled all of their food; and she ended with telling her exactly who the suspect was and how she found the victim, her brother – defeated and crying. Infuriated, my mother jacked me up as if I had committed a crime against her. With perched lips she winced in a deep, steady voice,

"tomorrow you gon' go up there and tear that lil' boy up, do you hear me?"

Without me responding she released me and told me to go clean myself up and get ready for dinner.

That night I did not sleep at all. This experience of being physically beaten up by someone had damaged my mind and spirit as much as my body but the thought of having to face that experience on command from my mother really rattled my soul. I had perfected the art of staying out of harm's way both at home and at school up until that point but that skill eluded me in this reality I was now living in. In my trembles of fear and restlessness, at some point during that night it came to me to pick up my Bible. I began sifting through it searching for stories that would provide me comfort and give me guidance on how to handle this situation that to me, in that moment, was a matter of life and death. My mother meant what she said and I knew it. I also knew, though, that I was only reading with three and a half eyes because the enemy that I had to face had already shut one of them half closed and publicly humiliated me.

I went through as many of the pages as I could, turning after just reading one line and not feeling inspiration. I must have flipped the pages 100 times that night but nothing helped me. I woke up the next morning to the routine sound of my mother screaming our names until we woke up. As I rose from my sleep I noticed the dead flashlight on top of my Bible underneath my hand that was covered in drool so the feather thin pages in my Bible were now welded together with my slobber.

Normally, our routine was for me to iron my own clothes before leaving for school and my sister would iron both hers and our little brothers. This morning my mom told my sister to iron my clothes, too, and ordered me to her room. As if she had eyes behind her back she told me to come to her the second my foot stepped on her carpet without ever seeing me. She ordered me to come closer to her and when I did she began lotioning my body with Cocoa Butter and then massaged Vaseline into my face forcefully as if she was preparing me for fight night in Vegas.

"When we get to that school I want you to point out that little boy who gave you a black eye and you better go up to him and do the same thing that he did to you. You hear me?"

"Yes, ma'am", I replied.

We got into the car and typically we would cruise to the sounds of Kem or R.Kelly behind the sound of mom talking on the phone. This morning, though the same sounds played, all I heard was just noise. The fear of what I was about to engage in scared me into that timid place I was so used to being in but then 'Jesus Walks' by Kanye West came on and I caught myself humming the words. Every other morning we hit all the red lights and the trip felt long but not this morning. It felt like we must have had a green at every stoplight and that my mom must have been going twice the speed limit because it felt as if we had arrived within a split second. My mom got out of the car with strong fury and purpose. Without saying hello, smiling, nor giving any other proper greeting all she said to the before-school program monitor was,

"I need to know who some lil boy named Ating is and why ya'll let him bully my son!"

Before I could even get to her all I remember hearing is my sister yell "there he go!". Immediately I felt heart palpitations and this 7th grade boy all of a sudden looked like one of those giant football players that I loved watching on Sundays except he wasn't just a player to admire from afar – he was a fierce opponent who I had just been obliterated by. I looked up at my mom and with those perched lips barely opening she squeezed out of her teeth the words, "you better go beat his butt". Again, I froze, but instead of the usual paralysis that I would experience I began to feel anger.

As if I was one of those cartoons on Madden and someone else was controlling me, I rushed my opponent and punched him square in the face. All I remember was the initial punch and everything else became a blur. Before I realized what had happened, I was standing over the boy with my hands scraped in his blood and his face leaking with the same. My mom, still filled with the same rage she started with wiped the tears from my eyes and told me to get in the car. I just knew that I was in trouble, but not from her. When she got back in the car, like a coach after a big play in a game she exclaimed,

"now that's what you do when somebody picks on you! Don't you ever let nobody touch you or your brother or sister, do you hear me?"

"yes ma'am" I replied, as my voice cracked with adrenaline, angst, and disbelief at what had just occurred.

"that's what you better do to anybody that mess with you!" she reinforced.

"yes ma'am" I replied, still shaking from the experience.

At some point on the way home a familiar gospel song came on. One that we used to always hear in Memphis but that I had not heard since we had arrived in Atlanta. As the song went on the tension in my body began to subside and I began to hum along.

"God has not given us a spirit of fear, but the Lord has given us! Power!

God has not given us a spirit of fear. But the Lord has given us!... Power"

In those moments I felt like David after he slayed Goliath.

The Source Revealed

I did not get any inspiration from my frantic reading the night before that fair ones with Goliath but at the time of action something had come over me. Even though I was in the fight I felt like I was watching from outside of my body. The moment was slow and I was overcome by something greater than my own might. My mom got back on the phone with whoever she was talking to as if nothing had happened, going on to praise me to her friend for what I had just done.

My mom let me stay home for the day so she dropped me off and went off to work. I spent the day reflecting on the morning I had and remember feeling like David after defeating Goliath but also like I had done something wrong. It was equal parts liberation of feeling like I had done a good deed, and sin like I had broken a commandment. I turned on NFL Streetz on my Playstation but before I could finish the game I felt the desire to open my Bible. In between the loading screen and the game starting I read scriptures and all of a sudden every word spoke to me like they had that summer before.

On that day I found this source of courage in the Bible and that was the last day I remember being shy and timid. The sin that I felt began to fade away as scripture began to take on more meaning to me and on this occasion, I felt validated by my mother who brought home McDonalds and a light energy that evening. It's as if everything had conspired to teach me this lesson of how to get over fear – and that was to face it! So I thought, at least.

The next morning from the time I woke up to the time I got to school my heart raced with the same fear I was accustomed to feeling. Again, all of the familiar sounds became just white noise and chatter. When we arrived to school I walked lightly hoping not to run into the boy who I had made bleed the day before but he was nowhere in sight. I went to my first class and tried to focus on my lesson but I was disturbed by whispering dialogue from classmates about what happened and notes being passed to me. I couldn't make out all that I was hearing and refused to accept the notes. I tried my best to tune it out and not think about what was still making me tremble but this distraction became stronger.

Right when the first period bell sounded I rushed to throw my things in my backpack and leave from class. I put my head down and tried to walk swiftly to my next class without being seen and as if he had spawned right then and there I looked up and there Goliath was walking in, face still bruised from our fight. When I saw him I did not feel anger nor fear but shame as if I had done something wrong. When he saw me he stood paused with an angry look on his face while mine was in shock. In what felt like a minutes long stare down we both stood unmoved and then he suddenly walked the other way.

As if the channel switched from gibberish to English on a TV, I was now able to decipher all of the chatter that was buzzing around me and it was about the fight that few saw but apparently everyone had heard of. By the time I got to class the stories from all the kids who were not there but had heard of what happened ranged from right to flat out wrong to highly exaggerated.

"I heard his mom made him fight Ating"

"I heard he and his sister jumped Ating"

"I heard he beat him with a chair"

It seemed like everyone was telling a different version of the same story. The pride I had the day before was revealed to be the pride of not having to face my mother because there was no pride in what I felt in school that day. Instead, it was guilt and shyness about everything that had transpired the day before.

When I went home that night I read my Bible again and this time with the focus on the Book of Samuel where I first heard of David and Goliath. Yes I had read it before but that book did not resonate with me in that initial pass because the context was not relevant to me then. But what was relieving for me in this moment was the feeling I got from knowing where to find that story. It was another feeling of validation. I was awakened by the sense of confirmation from this source and in that moment I realized how my source had been guiding me every step of the way this whole time.

I would be lying if I told you that on that day and in that moment I all of a sudden became this great conqueror that had no more failure. Hardly. What did happen that day was the revealing of a new routine for me. I finally knew exactly where to go when I was consumed by fear or anxieties and I put my routine to the test. For the rest of that year I walked past my Goliath, and though his face had anger sometimes, he never bothered me again and day by day I lost that tension that was once induced by his presence. I felt nothing at all towards him except the feeling that, even though he bullied me, I never wanted to do that to him. I was at peace and no longer timid in the face of fear.

Throughout that year I read my Bible and listened to College Dropout habitually and with each waking day the words that I read and listened to provided me with lessons to gain like never before. It was as if I had tapped into a part of my brain that I had never used prior.

Whether it was a bully, a hard class, a challenging conversation, a fear of failure, or something else, I now had a remedy. Over time my sources eventually became more than just the Bible and Kanye West that I would flee to when I needed the elixir of faith and motivation in times of trials and tribulations, but the good book and music that motivated me remained foundational staples for getting through life's challenges.

Before I ever thought about mental health or emotional health I thought about something bigger than myself that eventually began to empower me. Over time the results of my faith fortified my Mental & Emotional Health KPI and thus gave me belief that as long as I kept my mind on that which was good, good eventually would come and I know that it can do the same for anyone else with conviction. Good to me wasn't just what I had learned in the Bible but my studies of the Bible did provide a foundation for me to lean on almost automatically. Music provided the same for me and so did football and books, eventually, but this only came through my consistent interaction with these vessels of empowerment.

I began using music methodically to hype me up and to fill the silence, taking heed to the lyrics that naturally motivated me and inspired me into action. I ending up picking up football because I loved the sport, but it also gave me an outlet to which my Mental & Emotional Health KPI benefited greatly as a byproduct. Things did make me angry still but this sport allowed me an acceptable means to release that anger within the rules of the game. I read books as an escape and as a past time but the stories that I read were often times inspiring for me and relatable to various aspects of life. Books also gave me exposure to the world which further enabled me to keep my attitude of gratitude, aspire for more, and just keep pushing. Each source did something different but were equally impactful to how I channeled my emotions and what mental posture I approached situations with.

I'm not saying you have to read the Bible everyday or that you have to like rap, reading or football, but I do believe that the foundation to ensuring your Mental & Emotional Health KPI is stable is having a source to go to when you need a boost to both. Hopefully it goes without being said, but a healthy source, specifically. It can be family, a friend, a pet, a hobby, or anything you so choose. That's ultimately up to you but whatever it is you must practice the habit of engaging with it to feel the power of having confidence in it and be empowered by it. Just like with the relationship with money (or anything, as we mentioned), you want to have a relationship with this source in order to reap the greatest benefits of it.

The power of consistency cannot be understated, though. In a world where gratification comes much easier and sooner than in prior eras, this may cause frustration for some but I implore you to always keep a spirit of patience when it comes to identifying and building a healthy relationship with your source(s). The Bible was just something that I picked up at church every week. Then it became a book that calmed my thoughts. Eventually it became a source of empowerment. It did not happen overnight, though. It took years of developing a relationship with those scriptures and it took some trials before I knew what it was doing for me subconsciously. Delayed gratification may be tough to fathom but just like with your Physical Health and Financial Health KPIs, the power is all in our exposure and consistency of habits.

Mind Over Matter

This realization of the source that would fuel not only my courage, but my change in heart, went hand in hand with my ability to mind my thoughts and that ability went hand in hand with establishing a sound Mental & Emotional Health KPI. Life did not change overnight in terms of the external factors that troubled me. Middle school is a rough time period for most kids and I was no different. With two more school changes came it's share of similar threats. I didn't get bullied again because I never let it get that far but standing up for myself in the face of fear was a recurring theme in my adolescence. The courage that I needed to do so came not just from going to my sources but believing in those sources more than I believed in the fearful thoughts that would consume me prior to my David moment. The fear never stopped, but neither did the power of my sources when it came time to face a fear. Overtime the courageous thoughts overpowered the fearful thoughts and this was just the byproduct of building faith in my sources and developing a healthy relationship with them.

When I read empowering words in the Bible or any other book; when I heard empowering words from Kanye or any other artist or person, I internalized them. People still said and did hurtful things but that didn't matter as much as what I said and did to myself. No matter what mean or discouraging thing was said or inflicted, because of my relationship with my sources I knew something to tell myself that would override anything negative that came my way. No matter what failure or hurt came in life the Bible, other books, the rap lyrics I heard, football – they all gave me a counter-story or lesson to believe in during the bad days. Instead of dwelling on the bad, I developed a skill over the years to always focus on that which was good in life. This did not mean that bad evaded me, it meant that the bad did not impact me as harshly as it once did.

Many bad times in life were also remedied by the solace I found in my village. This, too, became one of my greatest sources. No matter where I moved to I was always blessed to have incredible friends that boosted my morale and spoke light into me on my dark days. On top of the tenacity and mental fortitude that I developed, my friends were lifelines for me that I cannot put into any amount of words. What I will say, though, is friends should supplement you – not make you nor destroy you. Having friends that were like minded in their approach to life was a cheat code that afforded me the privilege of befriending some incredibly successful people because behind most success is a strong ability to overcome failure. It's how you talk to yourself and about yourself. It's how you treat yourself and others. It's about your habits. My habits were to speak positivity into my life, to treat myself with kindness, and to form good, healthy habits. Thus I attracted people who also did the same and together we fed off of one another which undoubtedly contributed to my emotional and mental well-being in a positive way.

Because of my belief in God, I considered – and still do – that everything that happened was only partially due to my will but wholly according to God's plan so my attitude was always one of gratefulness that God gave me the sheer chance of life and that anything else to come was part of the greater plan for my life. My love for football went hand in hand with my faith and further aided my mental and emotional fortitude as well. Through much of my childhood I was obsessed with football. My mind was always on my favorite players and, like with most sports, football is a passionate game full of sage idioms, chants, and proverbs from coaches.

Football was my church in the wild. My coaches were pastors and us players were the pupils following our shepherds to the promise land of more wins than losses. They instilled a will in us to win and with it being a team sport, a will to compete not just for ourselves, but for the greater team. In high school we had a saying, "If it ain't rough it ain't right" so we grew a love for the tough battles because we saw proof that we could reap greatly only if we sowed greatly. Running everyday made us faster; lifting every day made us stronger; and repeating the same routes and patterns everyday made making plays second nature on game days.

We lived by the saying "Be brave, not stupid" which meant that it takes proper preparation to prevent poor performance. "Without preparation you're not brave, you're stupid", my coach would say. As a team we learned how to grow through the temporary suffering of two-a-days and that fortified our minds and literally our bodies into creatures that could withstand harsh elements, the physical pain, and mental libra scale of balancing life outside that gridiron and life within it.

As kids with just a passion to play the sport I don't think that we realized the life skills and lessons that our coaches were teaching us. They made us believe that it was a privilege to play this sport, so they held us accountable outside of the field to do what was necessary to ensure that we could play and not let our team down. The same mentality that it took to make it through early mornings, late nights, two-a-days, and the adversity that comes with trying to beat another team that wants to win as bad as yours was the attitude that I believe helped us all get through life at that time. To this day it's a core foundation of who I am.

Through my toughest trials as a child I could go run around and let out all of my emotions and truly feel ok to withstand the days that followed. Music was always playing so whether it was gospel, rap, or rock, the songs we would play in the locker room to hype us up were the same songs I would end up playing when I wasn't feeling up for the day or when I was too tired to study for an exam. The Bible was always where I went to get encouragement to find more reasons to believe that even through my stormy weather that I will reap great harvests for the seeds I've sowed so long as I don't let impatience or weakness keep me from sowing.

I kept my mind on those things night and day so those became my norms and the negative trials of life just became anomalies to me. It wasn't that I was any stronger mentally or emotionally or that I was just born with a heart of ice. It's that I kept my mind on just a few things that my world revolved around and found inspiration and positivity within them. When we lost on the field, or when I didn't do as well in class, or when things at home were going wrong, I still had my mantels of positivity to focus my mind on. My faith, my village, football, and music always gave me something to keep in mind to prevent the negativity from consuming me and I believed in those things like I believed in breathing. What I focused my mind on became what mattered. That is what strengthened my Mental & Emotional Health KPI, and if you can find those mantels for yourself I am confident that they can serve you just the same.

It Could Always Be Worse

A great benefit of having moved around so much in life was the exposure that I got. From days in the southside of Chicago to days living in the suburbs of Dallas I lived a great life overall. This doesn't mean it was void of some pretty bad times, though. One of my favorite books in the Bible, Ecclesiastes, talks about the "seasonality of life" and how there's "... a season for everything. A season for good and a season for bad." More than the beautiful truth in those words was the beautiful truth that life revealed of them for me.

Simply living life as I grew up living it has taught me that you could be living paycheck to paycheck, dependent on food stamps and welfare one year and in the next you can be feeding the homeless with your surplus of food and resources the next year for Christmas. It taught me that you could conquer every goal one month and be unsuccessful at all of your aims the next. It taught me that even after nasty storms that you could find a silver lining in the rainbows that gleam through the bright skies that follow. The seasonality of life always gave me reason to find something to be grateful for and a reason to just keep pushing. That *reason* for all of us to find gratitude is something that empowers our Mental & Emotional Health KPI to consistently trend positive.

I heard a wise person say that you're never as bad as people say but you're never as good as they say either. Those words speak to a duality in life that I find empowering. The reality of being grateful that things could always be worse and being ambitious towards becoming better created a means for me to always look at life in such a way that allowed me to tap into the best parts of myself. I believe that duality exists for us all and that it is our attitude towards life that augments either the good or the bad. I couldn't always prevent the fear that came nor the anxieties or bad thoughts, but over time that recipe of going to my sources and practicing gratitude allowed me to override those limiting, negative emotions and mental states with positive and empowering emotions and mental states.

How Gratitude Shows Up

My sophomore year in college I realized that life with football would end for me after I graduated so I began a passionate search for what it was that I wanted to do to be fulfilled in life. The benefit of being an athlete was that it allowed me to hone skills that were intangible – ones that my school curriculum did not necessarily teach. Skills like leadership, perseverance, belief, and posture. My college coach used to tell us, "how you do anything is how you do everything", so besides having to keep a passing GPA in order to remain eligible, I performed in class the same way I performed on the field – with diligence, focus, and with gratitude.

I developed healthy habits of studying material just as I studied film for football. I practiced my class problems just as I practiced routes and coverage. I persevered through my ignorance by following up with teachers just as I persevered through making a mistake on the field by discussing with my coach on the sideline. The parallels were easy for me to navigate because I was constantly reminded of the price tag of going to college and because my mom took out loans, I felt an extra push of motivation to make good on the investment she and others had made into me. Not to mention that, as I mentioned earlier, the internships that paid the most required the most so I was aiming high.

When stoichiometry and calculus III became the bane of my existence and I felt like procrastinating more than I felt like working I resorted to my second nature and found Bible scriptures in Ecclesiastes 11 to remind me that I am to be diligent with my time on this Earth and to be fervent with my efforts and I would call on a friend to study with. Whenever I had an opponent I would write a Bible verse on my wrist tape before suiting up and play my gameday playlist saying prayers as I went out to warm up. The Bible verses, the friends, the music, all reminded me that I was not only grounded by my sources but that I had so many reasons to be grateful.

I was grateful that I had the opportunity to attend college; I was grateful that I had friends who were equally yoked; I was grateful that I knew and was guided by God; I was grateful that I could play the sport that I loved to play. Gratitude did not always show up for me in every instance. I had to be enlightened by my sources to realize every way that I was blessed. What did it for me, though, was when I made a conscious effort to practice tapping into those sources habitually. Because I built that relationship with my sources every day it became second nature for me to find gratitude in most situations.

These habits that I consciously practiced early in life still form my habits today. When I started applying for jobs I did not apply for only places that I was *qualified* for. I went levels above and I never worried about the rejection or the failure because I knew that I would live to see another day. At the end of the day that is all that I needed to know and you should know the same. It's important to recognize that mental and emotional health is a continuum and that everyone experiences ups and downs in their emotional and mental well-being. Taking steps to promote good emotional and mental habits, such as maintaining social connections, seeking support when needed, adopting healthy lifestyle habits, and managing stress, can all contribute greatly to overall well-being. With healthy habits of building a relationship with my sources of empowerment and gratitude I truly believe the other piece of the equation is time because time heals most things when healthy habits are involved.

When All Else Fails Just Keep Pushing

So maybe sports aren't your thing nor religion or music. Maybe you never got to hear a wise person tell you that common saying of how *life is 10% what happens to you and 90% how you respond to it.* Maybe you never got inspiration from a pastor or coach or teacher. Maybe you've dealt with scenarios that make sports just what they are – a game – compared to what life has thrown your way. Whatever the case may be, your Mental and Emotional Health KPI, much like your Physical and Financial Health KPIs, come down to practices and habits and both of those require commitment and time. Reaching peak experiences of Physiological, Safety, Love & Belonging, and Esteem Needs in life can never occur without Mental & Emotional well-being.

I don't know all there is to know about Mental and Emotional Health but I do know that the power of the mind is much greater than the power of matter. It takes some forging, that's for sure, but our ability to achieve self-actualization in this life is dependent on it so no matter what you cannot give up! I don't want anyone to have to encounter physical violence or have unfortunate experiences to learn how to forge the fortitude to enable strong emotional and mental well-being but hopefully through the bits of my life that I have shared you can think about where your own sources come from and work on your relationship with those sources no matter where you are in life.

I share so candidly my experiences because I know too many people in this world who can resonate with my story. So many people who have had similar experiences and never got to grow through their experiences and keep their Mental & Emotional Health KPI in control. I share with hopes of inspiring anyone who needs inspiration to find that inner child that always needed something to make them feel safe, secure, and capable of conquering life's trials and tribulations and to equip them with all that they need to feel triumphant. My mom always says "at the end of the day the day gotta end" and when the day ends I want it to end only after someone finds what they needed in my experience of building Mental & Emotional Health.

Growth is never an overnight process. I, myself, have fallen short of the expectations that I had for myself plenty of times and I have certainly had days that just sucked due to no fault of my own. The key is to always find a way to examine your life and identify where you could progress even if it means just getting one percent better. Through tough situations I kept yearning to push forward and with each day that I was able to push forward that one percent started to add up and I know that it can for you, too. You just have to keep pushing even on the bad days.

KPI 4: Relationship Health

Healthy relationships are the cornerstone to all of our KPIs of Life and as humans we were made to have relations with one another. As we mature from fully dependent babies to independent adults, we never lose our need for a community of people who bring us love, belonging, and fulfillment. Maslow speaks to this in the Love & Belonging Needs, but I believe that healthy relationships with ourselves and other people impact everything from our basic physiological needs to self-actualization. Maybe it's family. Maybe it's friends you've known since childhood or people who've come into your life during different seasons. However these relationships form, they are special and essential to our well-being.

In the chapter on Financial Health I defined a healthy relationship as one that has consistently positive interactions; it promotes growth; and it does, in some way, mutually aid self-preservation. In the chapter prior I conveyed the necessity of 'building a relationship' with sources of emotional and mental strength. The same principles and controls apply here for our Relationship

Health KPI. Human to human relationships should be positive. This does not mean void of friction, but friction should not be detrimental. Likewise, healthy human relationships promote growth and positive experiences for each party. Depending on the nature and season of the relationship it is common that sometimes one party does more of the growth stimulation than the other, but the goal should be that both parties contribute to the other's betterment ultimately.

Another way to measure our Relationship Health KPI is on account of what impact it has on each party's physical, financial, mental, and emotional well-being. Relationships can be the source of both good and bad; peace and chaos; growth and stagnation, or worse degradation. That is reason enough to prioritize our Relationship Health KPI Relationships but doing so can look different for us all. Some people are introverted, others extroverted. Some like to be indoors while others like to be out. With all of the unique identities and perspectives each human has, our Relationship Health isn't easy to control – as they say, it takes two to tango. So long as you do your part of sticking to just a few core principles, though, you can position yourself to develop great relationships that will ensure your Relationship Health KPI is strong. These are those principles:

1. ALWAYS adhere to the Golden Rule of Life by following the Platinum Rule of Life
2. Don't just call people when you need them
3. Treat all people well but invest in people who want to invest in you
4. Improve the health of your other KPIs

The Golden Rule of Life

If we take a step back and ask ourselves *'what value does this book have?'* My hope is that the response is in the ballpark of: helping us to self-reflect on how we are doing at fulfilling our KPIs of Life at least; and at best, providing actionable steps to grow into a success. I was taught that the *Golden Rule of Life* is to treat others how you would want to be treated. As simple as that sounds it wouldn't be pessimistic to say that not everyone lives by this *Rule*.

You don't have to be the Pope or even religious to know that murder and theft are wrong, but what about the small things? Things like spurts of road rage or forgetting our friend's birthday or passing gas at your seat on an airplane instead of going to the bathroom? Turns out that what makes some have better relationships than others is actually those *small* things. In developing and sustaining healthy relationships it's not as simple as ruling out the big bad stuff. It most often actually comes down to those *small* things and that's the stuff that really tests and compounds the power of the *Golden Rule*.

I know a lady who goes by the name of "The Love Permissionist" and she hosts forums for discussions on various topics that encompass love and relationships. In one of her discussions that I got to participate in she spoke of love for our parentals – our mothers specifically – and in this forum she tasked us with something. After allowing people to share stories of their relationships with their mothers she asked us all to take a moment to think about our childhoods for 5 minutes. I sat there as the awkward silence of this Zoom call turned into a black hole of time that I was presently active in and before I realized time was up she says 'Now welcome back'. She then prompted us to enter a random breakout room where we were tasked with discussing the commonalities of our childhoods. The first moments here also felt awkward as no one knew where to start but then a lady from Chicago spoke up,

"Y'all remember walking to the candy lady house?" she asked.

Immediately, you felt the calm release fill this virtual space as if one hundred sighs were let out. Though most were not showing their face on camera, through the giggles and light-hearted idioms you could tell there were smiles on their faces just from the tone of their voices. One after another we all added onto this braveheart's intro. From funny things we laugh about now like parents saying "I'm doing this because I love you" before, after, or during chastisement. Or calling you into their room to grab something that would be literally right next to their body. To the same games we used to play and things we would eat even though we grew up in completely different states.

After about five minutes in this room the "Love Permissionist" brought us back into the main room and she asked a few members from each room to call out some of the things that were shared. As each room's representative spoke you could feel the warmth spreading as the faces you saw had smiles and the voices you heard had a childish tone. After the last group went she asked,

"Would anyone else like to share?"

After a few seconds of silence, in her calming voice that held this strong reflection only at the beginning of her sentences and at the end of them, the Love Permissionist said,

"And for all of these reasons you deserve to give and receive love in its highest form."

As I pondered on this session throughout the rest of my day a particular Bible scripture came to my mind:

"Love is patient and kind; love does not envy or boast; it is not arrogant or rude. It does not insist on its own way; it is not irritable or resentful; it does not rejoice at wrongdoing, but rejoices with the truth."

If you are Christian or have attended any American weddings you probably know this biblical verse because it is often recited during ceremonies. I've probably been to 30 weddings in my 30 years on Earth but it wasn't until this session with the Love Permissionist that those words truly resonated with me. When you define love in the same way that Bible verse does, how and to what degree we love can be easily measured. Because regardless of religion or ceremony, this definition of love is a universal benchmark for how we should treat ourselves and ultimately one another.

At it's root that Corinthians verse gives guidance to treat yourself and others in a way that is patient and kind and graceful, among other things. And if we really take into account that notion of "love in it's highest form" we can see how this definition fits all aspects of our lives. Even the little things. We would want someone to have patience with us on the road, someone thoughtful enough to remember our birthday, and we would certainly want our seatmate to be kind enough to go to the restroom to relieve their bowels.

Growing up in a household where typical childish behavior was punishable by brute force; playing sports that would quite literally penalize you for mistakes; and living in a world that is increasingly unforgiving in its judgements doesn't really set the best ground for learning how to be patient, thoughtful, and kind to ourselves. This then gets projected unto others and a vicious cycle begins.

I know firsthand, though, that combating these realities is possible and it starts with first doing the internal work to love yourself in that manner described by the verse in Corinthians. In turn you will find the humanity in the fact that if you can give yourself permission to be deserving of such a love then you can and should give that same permission to others. So if treating others as you would want to be treated is the Golden Rule, I would pose that this stance of giving yourself permission to love yourself in your highest form is 'the Platinum Rule.'

Adhering to this Platinum Rule is a simple idea but staying consistent at it has a learning curve. The way to combat that curve is through consistent awareness of *how* we practice adherence. Said differently, you have to manipulate your mind into being hyper focused on *how* you practice patience, consideration, humility, and the other tenets of love. My approach may sound self-absorbed but in practice it has proven to be highly effective. That approach is to always think about myself and how I would want something said or done to me.

If I were driving a bit slow, maybe because I had a child in the car or because I was lost or just because I was a cautious driver, I wouldn't want someone yelling at me and flipping me off so I think about that when I'm behind a driver going 45 mph on a 65 mph highway. When someone remembers my birthday and calls me or shows me love I think about that when I meet someone so I always ask their name and birthday. In situations where I expect to cross paths with this person again I often record their birthday in my phone so that I can provide them the same good feeling that I enjoy. When I encounter new people on the job and they get something wrong I quickly revert back to when I was in their shoes and recall how complicated I once found the task. This allows me to empathize and correct them in a way that is not belittling or discouraging. When I'm on a plane I wouldn't want to sit next to someone stinking up the joint so… well, you get the point.

Knowing how I would want to be treated grants me this baseline of how to treat others thus making the Platinum Rule more about understanding and knowing how to treat myself than others. If you practice patience, kindness, and consideration with yourself then how you treat others should be a reflection of that. People have little tolerance for people that do not treat them respectfully and rightfully so. Therefore, treating people how you would want to be treated is the foundation of developing healthy relationships and ultimately, ensuring you are developing a strong Relationship Health KPI.

So be mindful of the similarities in how you treat others versus how you treat yourself; also, be mindful of the difference. If you are treating yourself well, why are you not treating others at least just as good? If you are not treating yourself well then I hope that you give yourself permission to do so day in and day out. Life is better when we give ourselves and others the highest form of love that we all deserve.

Human Centered Over Transaction Centered

With every relationship that you have it is earnest work to ensure that the relationship is healthy while juggling all of life's other priorities as we grow. In my career as a consultant the most commonly used word, by far, is 'network'. Wanna win new projects? Network. Wanna get paid more? Network. Wanna build a better network? ...Network. Consultants, by function of the job, are some of the best people at building relationships of mutual benefit, or in other words, *networking*.

When I first started in my career it was a learning curve for me to get the hang of building relationships of 'mutual benefit' because by nature of the job you normally start off reaching out just to get something from clients. As I became more experienced, I realized the art of a pivotal skill that opened my eyes to how to see all relationships and it came back to those same words my mother would tell my siblings and I – "don't just call people when you need them."

Much like being at a top school or being in a professional sport, in the best consulting firms everyone is skilled and capable. As you start your career, though, you are not immediately entrusted with the responsibility of getting in front of c-suite executives and selling work to them nor do the large majority of professionals get to that point without significant development that comes from years of experiences. Not to mention there are already more senior professionals who came before you that hold that responsibility. As they win deals with clients they've spent years building a rapport with, it opens up opportunities for them to build teams full of junior staff to do the work.

Depending on the season, there can be more staff than open roles so getting the role that you want comes down to strategic alignment with those tenured account owners in order for them to know you well enough to choose you from the thousands of others options. It can be quite the learning curve to do this because the pressure of excelling turns most consultants into robots of the system whereby they treat interactions with people as just steps in their process to *climb the ladder*.

To some, relationships are seen as nothing more than transactional tasks. In fairness, the sport of consulting is no easy task. The sheer pace of client demands, the constant need to provide 'expertise' to nuanced situations, the politics of Corporate America, and the natural reality that you have to get your brand in front of as many people as possible to guarantee consistent work. Not to mention real life outside of work.

With all of this it becomes rather easy for consultants to only talk to colleagues in order to get a task complete or to get an example that they can leverage for their own use case. When it comes to dealing with tenured leaders or clients some only reach out to ask them about staffing opportunities while in between projects. In other words they take the 'human' out of human relations and replace it with 'transaction'. Many leaders see this and that's why they often have an inbox of 1,000 unread messages from people asking for favors and will only ever get to a handful of them. With a little emotional intelligence and a few months of observation early in my career, it quickly became apparent to me the fallacy in this way of working.

Having been in positions in life where I had more resources than others, I went through years of survivor's remorse where I felt it was my obligation to do for anyone that asked for a favor. I just knew I hadn't gotten anywhere in life alone and even if it wasn't the person requesting something, someone helped me so I felt it my duty to reciprocate this karma in life. Over time I began to dislike the feeling of only hearing from people when they needed something, though. In those cases where people who called for something never used my number for anything else it became something that I took personally because I began to feel like nothing more than a tool that they would use only when they needed.

As I grew in my career I noticed a similar trend not just with me but with others as well. On one hand I had people who would only send me an e-mail to ask for something. On the other were people who would call me just to see how my projects were going or to ask me if I could help them complete something they were already putting significant effort into. The latter became and are lifelong colleagues and, in many cases, close friends. The former, in many cases, had grown a reputation for this behavior and became easy to ignore. I have to believe that so many highly intelligent people were not "using" people on purpose so what was it then?

It all came down to what I call taking the transaction centered approach instead of the human centered approach. In the human centered approach, instead of asking for something first, I started by asking where I could help lend a hand. Instead of only looking to "network" when I needed a new job I introduced myself while I was already secured and focus on building a relationship built on learning about the other's interests, their work, and where they could use help.

Even the most generous giver can feel the burden of people who only reach out when they want something but never reach out to give of themselves with no expectation of receiving something in return. When you think of giving don't be too quick to think of giving as being superficial either. Knowing someone's birthday or their child's birthday or something significant about them is a powerful way to start developing a relationship. Most people who don't need anything from others often yearn for people who take a genuine interest in them or can augment the good in their life. The moment I picked up on this I vowed to incorporate this into all of my relationships and it has had an unanimously positive impact.

Instead of thinking of the transaction that I desired to take place I always focused on the person that I was interacting with in a genuine way. I never reached out to someone with a request first; instead, I always reached out to learn about the person initially. Conventional wisdom may think that this could get in the way of being productive but on the contrary, it actually boosted productivity in the long run. By taking this approach my network naturally began to expand as I took the time to invest in learning about others. This practice fostered a healthy relationship from the very beginning.

Before long I not only received desirable outcomes, but I often expedited the process of making other connections because the people I would interact with would connect me with people who they knew. Without deliberately trying I had built a rolodex of contacts who I knew and who knew me which helped immensely when it came to solving problems, acquiring knowledge, and in the case of work, staying staffed. As a bonus, work became more enjoyable and I was able to make friends, not just colleagues, while also generating great influence. Influence that kept me employed even during recession fears. Influence that put other people in positions to succeed. Influence that changed the trajectory of people's lives, including my own.

In the classic book by Andrew Carnegie *How to Win Friends and Influence People*, Carnegie catalogues over a dozen ways to do just that – make friends and build an influence. Out of all of the tried and proven methods, one that stands out as easiest for us all to do is to, as Carnegie puts it, "become genuinely interested in others". It's easy to get caught up in our own bubbles and with the seemingly unlimited access we have to others it's easy to perceive what others can do for us, but I challenge you to search for what you can do for others instead.

A true differentiator in this world is building relationships which means putting in the effort to sustain them. Don't ever be the person that only reaches out to their "friends" or family or anyone, for that matter, when you need something from them. If you haven't built a healthy relationship with people – one where you are mutually beneficial in some way – you can quickly become a burden and after a while you become the person that no one wants to answer the phone for. So a major key to ensuring that you have a strong Relationship Health KPI is to put humans first and not the transaction. Only then will you truly be able to build healthy relationships and sustain fulfilling those Love & Belonging Needs among other Needs.

Know Yourself to Know a Good Investment

If you want to know yourself, go spend time by yourself. Not time laying around and scrolling on your phone but time with just you and your thoughts. Think long walks at the park, or sitting down to gaze at the sky or look at the world in front of you. This is not an attempt to persuade on the effects of deep meditation or Monasticism, rather it is an impetus for how to live by those first two principles of giving yourself the highest form of love and prioritizing the person over the transaction. The serenity of solitude comes when you spend enough time with yourself to find out what makes you content.

Some people are introverts, some are extroverts, others are ambiverts. Depending on where you fall you may find it more natural to embrace this state of solitude or more difficult. In all cases, though, this time alone gives us our greatest exposure to who we are to ourselves and who we are to the world. This is important because it allows us to make the best determination of how others fit into our lives. Do the people around you give you more energy or less? Do you feel like you are progressing in life or staying stagnant with your current relationships? Do your relationships have mutual benefit? These are some of the questions that stem from first having a deeper understanding of yourself. With this realization it is my belief that no one has to feel alone and feel the need to invest in relationships that do not reciprocate value in some way.

Part of knowing how to love ourselves looks like knowing how to share our love with others within our own healthy and defined parameters. There's always room to treat everyone with respect, with kindness, and with good intent. There is also always room for limiting your interactions with people and prioritizing who you so choose based on your needs. There's a common belief that if you know the five closest people to an individual then you can get a good glimpse of who that person is. Your relationships with people and the health of those relationships have a direct correlation to your other Health KPIs – Physical, Financial, Emotional & Mental, and Esteem.

When you know yourself and know how to love yourself that is your first safeguard to ensuring that your relationships are mutually beneficial. What you require from others is a direct reflection of what you require from yourself so you can filter out what is healthy for you and what is not by simply answering the question of 'what do I need and what do I have to give'? There cannot be one without the other and the uncomfortable truth for many is that what you get has a direct correlation with what you give and that law of reciprocity is something to embrace!

With the knowledge of self that you gain throughout life experiences take inventory of the value that you bring people and augment that value by showcasing it everywhere you go. The other uncomfortable truth is that not everyone will find value in what you bring. As tough as that may sound for some, that should be of no concern to you. Your value is not dictated by another person's perception of it but it is an indicator of reality. Being able to read how people perceive you is a skill called EQ or Emotional Intelligence. EQ is the ability to both manage your own emotions and understand the emotions of people around you. That time alone goes a long way in managing your own emotions and being yourself goes even further in understanding the emotions of others, and you need both to reach those peak experiences in life and establish a sound Relationship Health KPI.

Emotional Intelligence helps you understand what relationships are worth investing in and if you take an honest inventory of that, it can also help you grow immensely as a person on your journey to reaching self-actualization. Think about some of the most loved people in the world. Maybe an athlete comes to mind or an artist. Maybe it's an author or someone of great influence. Whatever comes to mind, think about what makes people like them? Chances are it has nothing to do with what others give them; instead, it's often that those well-liked people give a lot to others. Whether it be the entertainment of excelling at their sport and giving fans a reason to cheer or maybe they are great at making the best songs to impact someone's mood or they give the best advice to make people feel more empowered. Whatever it is, it is more often than not because they give something of themselves to others.

You and I are no different – we all have some value to provide others and this world at large. When you find out what it is about you that you can give to others that is where your core of attraction lies. The balance of that gift that you possess – that we all possess – is that we must find the value reciprocated to ensure that it is sustainable. When it comes to your personal relationships, the health of them should be graded, in part, by the mutual benefit they bring. Those that bring the most mutual benefit, whether now or in the future, are the ones worth investing in and all others should become secondary to that at best.

The right relationships, the best ones, are priceless. The ones that make you better and that give you purpose are the ones worth investing in the most. These are the relationships that have the greatest power to positively impact your Relationship Health KPI. The disclaimer is in that old adage that good things take time, but be careful not to mistake your own patience for weakness nor another's. Not all great relationships have to start with cosmic chemistry right off the back. In fact, most great relationships take time to develop, in my experience.

With quality time spent alone you build enough knowledge of self to develop discernment for when time invested is up. Much like studying a stock – if you spend time analyzing it you can get a pretty accurate understanding of when the investment is no longer fruitful versus when it is just having a down period. When you do the due diligence of understanding yourself you get better at understanding your chemistry with others which becomes foundational to knowing if a particular relationship is worth the investment or not.

The Practical Law of Attraction for Relationships

The Law of Attraction is a popular philosophical and metaphysical concept that suggests, simply, that we attract whatever we focus our energy on – whether it be positive or negative. When it comes to relationships, this concept is battle tested. If you want to build relationships that value you, you must first value yourself. At its core, the law of attraction poses that like energy attracts like energy. So if you want relationships with physically healthy people then you must focus on being physically healthy yourself. If you want relationships with financially healthy people, then you yourself must focus on developing a healthy relationship with your own finances. I can keep going but I think that you get the point.

When you think about the relationships that you desire to have think about the qualities that they exhibit. Do you want relationships with people who work out, or who are funny, or who like to travel? Well, according to the law of attraction you must embody those attributes by focusing on them for yourself. In between what we have and what we desire to have is always a bridge that we have to determine how to cross. When it comes to relationships I never think it's best for people to do things just for others. Instead, I believe that we should act and do for what we believe will make us the best version of ourselves.

In that regard, I believe that the best way to build healthy and strong relationships is devote our energy towards ensuring we are the best versions of ourselves. To do that means to focus on ensuring we have healthy KPIs of Life. Our KPIs of Life are measures that are almost exclusively dependent on building controls that we can manage. As we have discussed in each chapter so far, each KPI has certain controls or principles, that if followed, have direct impact on promoting a healthy KPI.

As the Law of Attraction would suggest, when we focus our energy on being our very best a byproduct becomes the attraction of others who are working to become their very best! For this reason, I believe that the single most important thing that we can do to build a strong Relationship Health KPI is to prioritize optimizing each of our other KPIs of Life. To attract the best relationships focus on your Physical Health, Financial Health, Mental & Emotional Health, and your Esteem Health!

KPI 5: Esteem Health

Before reaching the pinnacle state of self-actualization, or the peak of Maslow's Hierarchy of Needs, you know there is the level called 'Esteem Needs'. By definition, Esteem Needs are our desires to have a stable and positive evaluation of ourselves and who we are in totality. But what does that mean? What does 'who we are in totality' mean? This comes down to the personal holy trinity – mind, body, and spirit. To obtain and sustain a strong Esteem Health KPI, or to have strong self-esteem, we must actively engage in filling our minds, our bodies, and our spirits with all that contributes to us being the best version of ourselves.

To piggyback off of a concept from the prior chapter, I like to think of having high esteem as having an ability to find fulfillment in ourselves by ourselves without any outside validation. It means that we feel good about ourselves; that we think good of ourselves; and that we see good in ourselves. That may come in the form of viewing ourselves as attractive enough, smart enough, or compelling enough just to name a few things. It may show up as being confident in what we stand on and what we bring to the world.

While self-esteem is intrinsically self-motivated, our Esteem Health KPI is highly dictated by what pours into each part of our whole being. Said differently, what we put into our minds, our bodies, and our spirit drives how our self-esteem comes to light. We all have self-esteem but we all channel it in our own ways. Some stronger than others and some more positive than others. The following principles are the foundations to fulfilling our Esteem Needs and ultimately positively impacting our Esteem Health KPI and overall self-esteem.

1. Find purpose
2. Be audacious in your vision of self
3. Have a SMART vision
4. Nurture and protect the mind, body, and spirit

Find Your Purpose or You're Wasting Air!

In the words of the late great, Nipsey Hussle, *find your purpose or you're wasting air!* I subscribe to a belief that we all have a purpose. I recognize the ambiguity in that since I do not know each and every person on Earth nor could I tell each and every person on Earth what their purpose is. I still believe this, though. So much so that I believe one's chief aim in life should be to identify that purpose and to live it out because without purpose why do anything? Just to live life by accident? Believing this truth is the first step in developing your Esteem Health KPI because when you have purpose, your self-esteem becomes directly linked to that.

I challenge you to do an experiment and go ask ten people the question: *who are you?* I'd bet you that after some visually apparent deep thought within the first few sentences, if not the first few words, they would mention something about their occupation, what they spend most of their day doing, and/or who they are in relation to their family. Whether that be a nurse, a student, an artist, a parent, or any other title, *what* we do often drives *who* we think we are. This, in turn, drives our self-esteem. To further prove this, I bet if you asked that same person to name something that they are proud of their response would be related to *who* they think they are.

This understanding of *who* we are is critical to understanding how to develop and enhance our Esteem Health KPI because knowing *who* we are allows us to assess who we are versus who we want to be. That gap is where our esteem needs lie and those needs define what we need to fulfill in order to build up a good Esteem Health KPI. Said differently, our esteem needs are the needs that we must fulfill in order to reach that audacious and worthwhile goal of becoming everything that we want to be in life. More important, our Esteem Health KPI is a direct indicator of how well we are doing at fulfilling those esteem needs.

In so many words what I am conveying is that our esteem relates to the worth we place on our lives. That is not to say that all people with high self-esteem deem themselves more worthy than others, but it does mean that when they look in the mirror they see someone that deserves good things to happen to and for them at a bare minimum. It means that they know that they are worthy of being respected and valued; not more than others, but certainly not less.

When you walk and live in your purpose it must be held in high regard in order to have a positive impact on your self-esteem. Just having a purpose means nothing if that purpose is not looked at with some level of gravitas or importance because without that belief that your purpose is a serious matter it becomes susceptible to be devalued and given up on by yourself. When this happens the Esteem Health KPI takes a big hit so you always want to protect purpose from all forces – both internal and external.

As I mentioned in regards to the Relationship Health KPI, humans we need other humans; but it should not be at the detriment of our own feelings towards and about ourselves. The disclaimer

I must make as it pertains to dealing with others and their realization of your purpose is that your purpose is just that – yours. While having people that believe in it can be helpful, other's belief should not be a factor in discovering and determining your purpose. In fact, even with the belief of others your own belief in your purpose should be the strongest and most important. By all means, though, I would say to stay far away from those who do not believe in your purpose. Especially as you begin discovering and living out your purpose as it is common that your faith in self may not be at its optimal strength when you start out. That's natural.

Purpose does not have to look conventional or the same as anyone else's but it can certainly be the exact same as someone else's. There's not just one author or one doctor in the world and likewise there is always room for you to contribute in any lane that you feel compelled to, and you are never confined to just one. So often we believe and are confined to the thought that we can only serve one purpose in life, but we are humans! The most complex and advanced creatures on planet Earth – it is virtually impossible that we only have one skill or just one thing that gives us energy and purpose. If you don't know your purpose I always find value in sharing two of my favorite Bible verses as a means to identify it; they are verse from Ecclesiastes and Colossians (9:10 and 3:23, respectively). The first states – *"Whatever your hand finds to do, do it with all your might for in the realm of death there is no place for Earth's work".* The second states – *"Whatever you do, work at it with all your heart, as working for the Lord, not for human masters, since you know that you will receive an inheritance from the Lord as a reward."*

As a believer, these verses empower me to appreciate that life is a gift and that with that gift I can work towards whatever I want while I have the time. It also empowers me to know that giving my best effort is a form of gratitude, so whether I am cleaning my dog or writing a book, I want to do my best! This did wonders for me because after realizing that I would not fulfill my dream of going to the NFL I did not know what my passion nor purpose was. I did have a desire to make money which helped fuel what I pursued next, but more than that was this habit of showing gratitude by doing everything to the best of my ability. That is how I discovered my passion for writing, for finance, for traveling, and eventually for finding my purpose in helping fill voids in the world.

I want to emphasize, though, that passions aren't always the things that bring us money or what we take a major in either. I majored in Physics and Industrial Engineering and I have never worked in either field professionally. Instead, passions are the things that brings us joy or a sense of fulfillment when we do them. If you haven't found your passion I encourage you to try different things and really try them! The things that give you the best feelings will inevitably lead you to your passion(s) and purpose(s). I found a passion for solving the problems dealing with numbers by working hard in all of my classes; I found a passion for writing in trying to better myself by writing my goals and thoughts down; and I found my passion for traveling by finding constantly going outside of my comfort zone in pursuit of opportunities to challenge myself and grow. So if you are struggling to find your place in life, have no fear. As long as you have breath you have an opportunity to give each day your all until you discover it.

What living out our purpose does to our self-esteem cannot be articulated in a way that does service to actual feeling. Living out your purpose makes getting out of the bed exciting. It makes conversations with people more meaningful. It makes each move more calculated, and thus, examined. Living out your purpose brings a clarity in life that almost forces you to walk with high self-esteem and that is powerful! Finding your purpose will always lead you to having more control of your Esteem Health KPI so if you want to optimize this KPI start by finding what it is that you find purpose in doing.

The Audacity It Takes

Faith without work is dead and that is why finding something purposeful is quintessential to not just our Esteem Health KPI, but all of our KPIs of Life. That sense of purpose alone has the power to drive you to act and after finding purpose the most important thing to do is act on it. I want for everyone to act boldly in their purpose though, for our level of audacity towards our purpose is one way to ensure that we have a strong Esteem Health KPI.

Your purpose should feel larger than one life and that may feel scary or nerve wrecking, but be careful not to detract yourself because of this. If you've ever heard the quote, "if your dreams don't scare then they're not big enough" I am here to affirm that saying because when I speak of audacity that is inherently what I meant. Audacity means boldness and bold things often evoke feelings that invigorate and sometimes cause trembling emotions even. That's the stuff that can keep you awake at night; that can fill you with thoughts of 'what if I fail'? This same feeling can also intimidate others and, worse, fill others with doubt or even envy.

Do not confuse the feeling with fear, though. It is simply a natural human response related to what is called *fight or flight*. When faced with great challenges, which audacious goals are, it is human nature to either fight for achievement or fly towards safety and comfort. In this case always fight for achievement because in that pursuit there is no such thing as failure or loss. It is only faith forging and lessons that come from fighting for your most audacious goals and dreams and the outcome is always greater fulfillment of our esteem needs which in turn result in a stronger Esteem Health KPI.

As I mentioned before, part of finding purpose comes out of a kind of humility that recognizes the servitude and gratitude in our efforts. I heard a quote once that said, "if you don't know what choice to make then make the hard one." Now I won't ask the analytical minds to poke the obvious holes in that quote but, as I tend to do, I did take notice of the good from such a statement. In this case, as it pertains to our natural fight or flight instinct, it serves as a powerful slogan to drive our audacity and choose the harder act of fighting for rather than fleeing from our biggest aspirations and goals. Because on the other side of the uncomfortable parts of life is always glory and purpose.

To know that I have a purpose and to want to fulfill that purpose gives me what the French call a *raison d'etre*, or one's most important reason to exist, and there's great power in that. The power in knowing why you exist is not just a selfish merry-go-round of thoughts; it's actually rooted in altruism – or it should be if you buy into the first sentence that I wrote in this section, "...we all have purpose". If and when you find your purpose it should come to you as a good thing. When we have an audacious, or bold, vision of who we can be our esteem needs come from the pursuit of bringing that vision to fruition through the setting and achievement of SMART goals that align to a SMART vision.

SMART Goals

I mentioned SMART goals briefly before but I want to take a moment to define this acronym for anyone unaware. SMART goals are goals that are *specific, measurable, achievable, relevant, and time-bound (SMART)*. When it comes controlling the health of KPIs of Life, setting goals should be common practice but not just any goals – you have to make them SMART. In other words, a goal must first be specific to you and your purpose. So much so that you should be able to articulate it clearly and specifically. Your goals must also be measurable in a quantitative or qualitative way so that you can track your progress clearly. Goals must be achievable such that reaching it feels possible to you in some logical way. They must be relevant so as to align with your purpose in life or the purpose that it relates to. Lastly, your goals must be time-bound. Meaning they must have a definitive start and end time-frame so that you can assess them based on where you are and where you intend to be at completion.

As an example, if you determine that your purpose in life is to teach then one of your SMART goals could be constructed following this logic:

- You first want to first *specify* what it is that you want to teach so let's say finance for this example.
- After determining that specific subject, you can make it *measurable* by setting a number of people you aim to teach or a degree to which you want to teach the subject. Is it 10 people or 10,000? Do you want to teach kindergarten or do you want to teach college level?
- If you say that you want to teach 10,000 people then you next must determine how *achievable* that is based on where you are today.
- Because you said that your purpose is to teach the sheer fact that you are aspiring to live out that purpose through the subject of math makes the goal *relevant* by itself.
- How achievable the goal is goes hand in hand with the *time-bound* aspect of the goal in this case. If your goal is to teach 10,000 people by tomorrow then that becomes a different level of achievable compared to teaching that many in a year.

- Setting that time-bound aspect out to a year makes it considerably more achievable compared to a day so you could decide to give yourself a year to achieve the goal.

The power of setting SMART goals is two-fold as it relates to our Esteem Health KPI. On one hand it enables and requires you to think critically about your goals which is a great thing because that requires intentional thoughtfulness and effort. This promotes you to empower yourself by dreaming big! Equally as important as thinking critically and dreaming big, setting SMART goals are meant to build your esteem. By setting SMART goals you are actually creating esteem needs that, when fulfilled, positively impact your self-esteem and overall Esteem Health KPI. That is the great correlation!

With every goal that you set for yourself you are also setting a *need* that you want fulfilled either as an outcome of the goal or as a byproduct of pursuing it. Feeding your vision with positive affirmations from yourself and others also drives positive effects to your self-esteem so being intentional about how you talk about your SMART goals and who you talk about them with becomes critical especially if you are starting fresh. The only thing better than having people who believe in you is having a greater belief in yourself and that is something that you develop through creating and accomplishing your SMART goals. That is why, at principle, I believe so vehemently in the practice of setting SMART goals.

This simple action, if done consistently, has the power to transform your life in just a year. If you have never tried it, be my guest! I am certain you won't regret it! So much of our Esteem Health has to do with our own ability to find value within ourselves and even if it is something as simple as making your bed every morning or starting your day with a cup of water, making a habit of setting goals and accomplishing them is one sure way to boost the value you see when you look in the mirror.

Mind, Body, and Spirit

When we realize the important purpose of a healthy mind, body, and spirit we take care of those facets of our existence. Similar to that favorite pair of shoes, or pants, or watch that gives us a sense of confidence and worth we ensure that it is not just cleaned but looked after. We reserve a certain place in our closet for it, we assign it for important occasions, and we see to it that it fits or works properly. The same applies to one's self-esteem. When you live a life of purpose you find a reason to be intentional about taking care of your Esteem Health or what makes you feel a sense of worth!

An important component of our worth is the sustainment of our mind, body, and spirit because together they work to satisfy the perspective we have of ourselves. When the mind is sharp our thoughts are sufficient enough to identify solutions to our problems and, even better, to boost our self-esteem from within our minds. When the body is taken care of we have the strength to overcome obstacles, sustain life more comfortably, and superficially boost our self-esteem. When the spirit is grounded in good substance we are empowered to rise to any occasion and handle any trial or tribulation with grace and spiritual fortitude. This does not mean that we will be void of failure, but it does mean that we are capable of not being defined by the failures. When all three facets are well taken care of we become unstoppable because we cannot be broken! That is the importance of maintaining and sustaining a strong mind, body, and spirit as it pertains to your Esteem Health KPI. With the upkeep of that holy trinity we forge a strong self-esteem.

To see to it that we are keeping the mind, body, and spirit fortified we must protect what enters all three and that happens by culmination of all that I have shared in this book. To ensure a fortified mind we must influence what goes into it by exposing ourselves to positive and dependable sources of perspectives. This looks like speaking positive affirmations to ourselves, surrounding ourselves with people who have a positive impact on us, and putting forth our best effort to be mentally strong. All things done by maintaining good Relationship Health and Emotional & Mental Health. To ensure our bodies are fortified we must ensure we put good substance into it and consistently work it under good stress. This looks like eating a nutritious diet, working out regularly, and practicing self-preservation. All things done through maintaining good Physical Health and Financial Health. And to ensure that our spirits are fortified we must devote significant time developing a relationship with the sources that empowers it. This looks like spending time alone with our sources, meditating on the things that we need and desire, and putting our best foot forward in every walk of life. Also things done by maintaining good Relationship Health, Mental & Emotional Health, and Esteem Health.

Building esteem, like building relationships, is hard to subscribe a cookie cutter methodology to but throughout my life I have found positive effects when adhering to the principles and habits I have laid out within this chapter. In a world that is filled with infinite amounts of content and exposure to a vast range of things both valuable and useless, the one thing I must also emphasize is the need for focus! If you've ever checked your screen time that can be a good start at getting real about your focus. I speak with many people on this topic of self-esteem and while I have done no scientific studies, I have found an interesting correlation between those who tell me they struggle with self-esteem and high amounts of screen time. In one instance I met with a young lady who was averaging over 15 hours per day on her phone!

The power that many of us have in the palm of our hands is often no more than an infinite distraction tool that we use to mindlessly fool around with and clog our minds and spirits with unnecessary noise. That same tool can open up the doors to a life of endless positive exposure and promoters of growth, though. I find it more and more common that youth and even many adults battle depression and I can't help but recognize this as a side effect of social media. I think social media has done a fantastic job with making us feel more connected and providing exposure at a level never seen before in history. In the same breath, though, I also have to say that it has contributed to the rise in people feeling less connected and anxious because of over exposure.

Never before in history has a generation had so much to process so while that has brought much good, unfortunately it has brought out some pretty bad ramifications as well. If you find yourself struggling with improving your Esteem Health I would challenge you to check your screen time and start putting limits on how much you consume on your phone. Replace the mindless scrolling with learning through reading or watching something educational. Go out to events with people and leave your phone on silent. Practice having conversations with strangers. Do something to detach yourself from scrolling on social media apps. What you focus on has an incredible impact on what you see – remember the *Laws of Attraction!*

If you focus on things that do not push you towards your purpose then by default you focus on that which pushes you away from it. When you're away from your purpose it is easy to lose quality self-esteem because you are probably becoming lost in life simply because you strayed from your purpose! So while following the principles shared throughout this chapter is a good foundation for you, that foundation won't be strong without the correct level of focus and devotion to the substance of that foundation. All of these controls will enable you to keep that focus, though, and optimize your Esteem Health KPI.

Where Self-Actualization Occurs

Up until I took got to college, where I was exposed to Maslow's Hierarchy of Needs, I only had one real vision of success and through football is how I dreamt of achieving it. I spoke of Maslow's Hierarchy of Needs throughout this book because it is the foundation of my own ideology of how to 'succeed' in life. You can say because of this ideology, I was able to define success in an actionable way.

Post high school can be a scary time for many people, even the most prepared, and I was no different. Realizing football would end for me once I finished college, where I was racking up some student loan debt and experiencing the bare minimum in life as a college student, I grew anxious about the future. Looking back, you could even say I grew unhinged. Learning about this Hierarchy of Needs, though, helped me to solve my conundrum by shifting my perspective.

What I mean is that my perspective on life began to shift from a focus on the end state to a focus on the path. Before that awakening I just believed that football was the only thing I loved to do and that it paid millions if you went to the league. Of course, I thought of the house I could buy my mom and the car I could buy my pops and all the things I could do. I never focused on what that meant on a day to day basis nor how I could bring these same thoughts to fruition outside of playing football. If you ask any former athlete they would probably tell you of a similar crisis that they experienced as they transitioned from their sport. It's a painful and scary feeling that leave many *stuck* and *lost* in life.

Now I cannot tell everyone *how* to be successful because I don't know what success means to everyone. What I can tell everyone, though, is that we all have a Hierarchy of Needs or what I call *KPIs of Life*. You may not call it 'Physiological' or 'Love & Belonging' needs, but we all have desires to live in a secure home and have food on our tables. We all want to be around people who we love and who love us. Even when we are not our best selves, we all still deserve the opportunity to feel a sense of pride in who we are. These desires are what make a life worth living.

At the core of my desire to play football was a desire to be able to fulfill my own Hierarchy of Needs. It was a means for me to afford the food that I needed and wanted; a means to live where I wanted to live; to secure myself and my family; to have a schedule that was flexible enough to allow me to enjoy time with my family and friends; to go wherever I wanted to go; and to make a difference in the lives that I came in contact with. Through the perspective I gained from Maslow's Hierarchy of Needs I realized that, in essence, playing football was simply a means for me to reach self-actualization. Maybe more importantly, through this perspective I realized that playing football was only but one way. Certainly not the only way. That discovery made all the difference.

The beauty in this Hierarchy of Needs is that it made me realize that playing football was a journey to an end and that there are always multiple paths to reach the same end. That was the magical shift in perspective that saved my life. I came to realize that playing football was only something to fulfill my Esteem Needs and that multiple things fulfilled my Esteem Needs. When I would help kids, conquer a tough real world use case in class, travel to a new destination, live by the words I read in the Bible, or slip a few hundred dollars in my mom's purse I felt the same sense of purpose and pride I got from football. It was this good feeling like I was doing something right in life.

As I entered my career I realized that I had opportunities to fulfill those same needs by doing things like volunteering, on behalf of my company, to be an instructor for kids at Junior Achievement. Similarly, as I learned about stocks I wanted to know how to model my desired investments as a challenge to my gut feeling. Working in banking afforded me free opportunities to learn and practice the skills to do this. With these skills I also found opportunities to get jobs that would pay me to do this. With that earned income I was able to fulfill my financial needs and build good Financial Health. My career also allowed me opportunities to travel to different cities and countries on the company dollar. The icing on the cake, though, was that my career also afforded me the ability to try and pay my mom back for all of her sacrifices. All of these things helped me to fulfill each of my KPIs of Life, which validated my perspective that there were more means to the ends that I desired.

I am not sure what exactly self-actualization looks like for you in the end but my aim in all of this was to help you see clearly the journey to reaching it. Ensuring you are fulfilling your KPIs of Life is equated to how you meet your own Hierarchy of Needs and ultimately reach self-actualization. That is the definition of success. Through the principles and practices that I shared it is my hope that anyone who needs a clear blueprint for how to fulfill their own needs finds it in these specific and connected key performance indicators that you can look to and measure yourself against. When we can fulfill our KPIs of Life we reach peak experiences in life that allow us to grow and that growth gets us closer and closer to that beautiful place of self-actualization.

In this sport of life don't forget that these KPIs are not something that is one and done. Na, LeBron and MJ didn't become great just because they had one good season. You have to see these KPIs as benchmarks that must be developed and sustained over time. If you have ever heard of the concept of getting 1% better every day or 'continuous improvement' then you know that change can seem small everyday but immense when measured over broader gaps of time. Where self-actualization occurred for me was in realizing the growth I have made and continue to make each and every day no matter how small. It occurred in not just discovering my Key Performance Indicators but discovering how to improve those KPIs with each period by which I measured them. That's where I found the growth. That's where I found self-actualization. From my perspective that's where I found success and where I believe you can, too.

About the Author

Will Everett is a Finance Consultant and Career Coach who finds the synergy in a true work-life balance by showing up as his authentic self and helping others to do the same. As a graduate of both Morehouse College and North Carolina A&T State University he began developing his passion by living by the words "lift as you climb". In this light he has achieved many professional accolades but what he has valued most is opening doors for others. As a past Dallas-Ft. Worth Morehouse College Alumni Chapter president he has helped raise over $30,000 dollars for aspiring college student from the DFW area. As a founding Board Member of Make A Play Foundation he has been a part of the transition of over 1,000 collegiate student-athletes into professional careers at some of the largest and most prestigious Fortune 500 companies including Goldman Sachs, Accenture, Morgan Stanley, and more.

Today Will resides in Houston, TX where he lives with his wife and dog, Barack. In his spare time he enjoys traveling, spending time with his family and friends, and worshiping at Wheeler Avenue Baptist Church.

www.ingramcontent.com/pod-product-compliance
Lightning Source LLC
Chambersburg PA
CBHW030452100526
44580CB00006B/101/J